CREATIVE CUISINE MINCEUR

Low Calorie French Cooking for Beginner and Expert

RUTH KNIGHTON MALINOWSKI

WEATHERVANE
BOOKS

PICTURE CREDITS

The following pictures were provided through the courtesy of Transworld Feature Syndicate, Inc.:

Syndication International: pp. 33 42 50 83

Lennart Osbeck: pp. 61 99 109

Michael Holtz: p. 54

Euphot: pp. 92 & 93

Studio Conti: p. 14

Library of Congress catalog card number: 77-77812
ISBN: 0-517-225174
Published under arrangement with Ottenheimer Publishers, Inc.
Printed in the United States of America.

Contents

introduction

creative cuisine minceur

The latest approach to French cooking is called "la cuisine minceur," a phrase derived from the adjective "mince," meaning "slim." This new slimming cookery has opened the way to the development of many new and delicious dishes. An added benefit is that these foods cut down on two enemies of good health: excess calories and cholesterol.

This new method of cooking has been called a cuisine of simplicity as compared with "la grande cuisine" (the great cuisine) which has been popular in France for centuries. Customary rich sauces have been eliminated in favor of preserving and enhancing the flavors and juices of the natural ingredients.

Although many chefs have recognized a need for less lavish and rich meals, Paul Bocuse and Michel Guerard, two well-known French chefs, are probably the persons responsible for this new style of cooking. These chefs discovered that good taste does not mean saturated fat, cholesterol, sugar, and salt. They have developed new techniques and borrowed practices from other ethnic cuisines to change traditional French methods of cooking. You will recognize some of these techniques, especially certain Chinese cooking skills, as you prepare these recipes.

Cuisine minceur was developed on the premise of eliminating or minimizing the use of high-calorie ingredients. This means using no butter, no oil, no cream, no sugar except natural sugar in fruits, no starches, no eggs, and no alcohol unless the alcohol content is evaporated. Since many of these restricted foods also contain high amounts of cholesterol, there is a double benefit. Some chefs follow the basic rules very strictly and never use these items. However, most chefs use some of these ingredients occasionally and sparingly. Now good food can be accompanied with good health.

Although the new French cooking is called a cuisine of simplicity, it does not take less time in the kitchen than the old "la grande cuisine." (Here simplicity refers to the use of natural flavors.) Most of us in the United States do not have the desire or the time to spend long hours on our food preparation. However, this book presents recipes that meet the general principles of cuisine minceur, but are easy to prepare and not time-consuming. Recipes are given that are international in taste and tradition.

Please note that this is not a weight-reduction book. However, if these recipes were followed and the principles applied to other daily cooking, one could very well lose weight and maintain lower cholesterol levels. But that is not the intention of this book. The emphasis here is on eating digestible, light, flavorful but natural, healthy foods; you will be able to eat well without gaining weight.

principles

Always buy and use the freshest ingredients possible. Traditionally, French cooking has been based on the use of fresh, natural ingredients. Only 30 percent of the French diet is composed of processed foods as compared with over 50 percent of the United States diet. Of course, during certain times of the year, frozen foods may be a better quality than fresh foods.

Eliminate or lessen the quantity of certain high-calorie or high-cholesterol ingredients.

Fats and oils: Completely eliminate butter and cream. Since small amounts of polyunsaturated oil or margarine may be used, look for nutritional labelings to help identify which margarines have more grams of polyunsaturated fatty acids. Note: Tub margarines are always more unsaturated than stick margarines. Avoid peanut and olive oils which are not polyunsaturated and therefore are less desirable. (Call or write your local Heart Association to obtain a current list of the most unsaturated margarines.) Also, meats and fish should be chosen carefully: Select lean meats and trim off the fat; chicken and turkey are good choices; most shellfish, non-oily fish, and white fish such as sole, halibut, and flounder are good selections for cuisine minceur fish recipes. Stay away from fat fish such as herring, mackerel, and tuna.

Egg yolks: Since egg yolks are high in calories and cholesterol, they are not included in cuisine minceur recipes. An exception is made for recipes such as bread, where the quantity of egg yolk per person is very little.

Flour: Eliminate or reduce flour and other starches. Flour itself is not high in calories or cholesterol, but it is traditionally used with fat to create calorie-heavy sauces. In this book only small amounts of flour or starch have been used for necessary techniques such as binding ingredients or thickening certain sauces. Although most French chefs do not include bread in a cuisine minceur meal, I feel this category of food can be very nutritious. Generally, the spreads that are put on the bread contribute most of the calories. The bread recipes included in this book are especially wholesome and interesting.

Sugar: Eliminate or cut down on all sugars. (These include table sugar, brown sugar, maple syrup, and honey.) In cuisine minceur, many fruits, which provide their own natural sweetnesses, are used for salads and desserts. Desserts in this book have been developed with reduced quantities of sugar. Although the taste may seem more tart than usual, a preference for this natural taste will develop over time.

Salt: Reduce salt intake to allow flavors from herbs and spices to be tasted. Our present United States diet provides much more salt than is necessary for body functions. A recent Senate committee report suggests that salt be reduced by 50 to 85 percent in our diets.

Cheese: Choose cheeses that are low in fat to avoid high calorie and cholesterol contents. Cheeses used in these cuisine minceur recipes are low-fat cottage cheese, ricotta cheese, and mozzarella cheese made from skim milk. These cheeses often substitute very well in place of higher-fat cheeses. In recipes that require the flavor of higher-fat cheese, the quantity of the richer cheeses has been reduced to a minimum.

special techniques

Sautéing: Pan-frying (sautéing) foods in a large amount of fat or oil is completely out in cuisine minceur. If oil is used at all, it is cut to a minimum. Amounts of oil or margarine could be reduced further by using a teflon-coated pan or a cookware spray. In some recipes sautéing is done by using small amounts of water or wine to cook and soften vegetables. Also, some foods cook very well in a tightly closed container over low heat without any added liquid.

Stir-frying: Stir-frying is an Oriental cooking technique used often in cuisine minceur cooking. A small amount of oil is heated and one food at a time is stirred and lightly tossed in the hot oil until done. If a wok is used, the cooked food can be pushed up the sloping sides to stay warm while other foods are stir-fried. In other pans, the food is removed until all stir-frying is completed. Then foods are combined and a sauce is added.

Thickening sauces: This is not done by the classic method of using butter and cream. Instead, juices are reduced to a natural gravy by raising the heat and evaporating excess moisture. This technique preserves the natural flavors of the basic ingredients. If a sauce needs more body, yogurt may be stirred in during the final step.

Deglaze: A technique of adding small amounts of liquid such as wine to the natural residues in the cooking pan is often used to capture the natural flavors in a quick cuisine minceur sauce.

Use of fresh herbs: Try to use fresh herbs, if possible, for a flavor treat. Most dried herbs lose much of their aromatic qualities after a year of storage. Because most Americans have more access to dried herbs, the recipes in this book generally use dried rather than fresh herbs. Usually ½ to 1 teaspoon of dried herbs equals 1 tablespoon of fresh herbs.

Special equipment: The use of special equipment should not be necessary for cuisine minceur cooking. Use your imagination and utilize your present appliances. Electric woks, skillets, crockery pots, steamers, and claypots may be used for many recipes in this book.

health and cuisine minceur

A recent Senate committee report urges Americans to make drastic changes in their diets. The over-consumption of fat, particularly saturated fat, as well as cholesterol, sugar, salt, and alcohol have contributed to heart disease, cancer, cerebrovascular disease, diabetes, arteriosclerosis, and cirrhosis of the liver.

Cuisine minceur was developed by persons concerned with their health and at the same time insisting on good-tasting foods. Although the principles for cuisine minceur vary from chef to chef, I have selected the best of these techniques and principles to cut down on calories and cholesterol. These recipes also provide good taste from fresh natural ingredients.

appetizers

eggplant appetizer

Yield: 4 servings

> **1 medium eggplant**
> **1 onion, minced**
> **2 tomatoes, peeled and seeded**
> **½ teaspoon salt**
> **¼ teaspoon black pepper**
> **1 clove garlic, crushed**
> **1 tablespoon lemon juice**
> **1 tablespoon wine vinegar**
> **2 tablespoons vegetable oil**
> **2 tablespoons dill, chopped**

Bake eggplant at 375°F until softened. Cool, peel, and chop. Place in cheesecloth or sieve and press out excess water. Place in blender with rest of ingredients and blend until mixture is smooth. Season to taste.

Chill and serve as a dip for fresh vegetables or on Bibb lettuce as a first course.

crab-meat spread

Yield: About 1¼ cups

> **1 can (7½ ounces) king crab meat,**
> **drained and flaked**
> **1 teaspoon prepared horseradish**
> **½ teaspoon seasoned salt**
> **¼ teaspoon lemon juice**
> **Dash white pepper**
> **½ cup plain yogurt**

Combine crab meat, horseradish, seasoned salt, lemon juice, and pepper. Fold in yogurt. Cover and chill.

Use to spread on crackers or as a dip.

garden dip

Yield: About 1¾ cups

⅔ cup low-fat cottage cheese
1 tablespoon finely grated onion
1 tablespoon finely grated carrot
1 teaspoon finely chopped green
  pepper

½ teaspoon salt
Dash garlic salt
1 cup plain yogurt

In a small bowl, mash cottage cheese with fork. Add onion, carrot, green pepper, salt, and garlic salt. Beat until fairly smooth. Stir in yogurt. Cover and chill several hours.

Serve as a dip with chips or raw vegetables.

confetti dip

Yield: About 1¾ cups

1 package low-calorie Italian
  dressing mix
¼ cup chopped cucumber
¼ cup finely chopped green
  pepper

¼ cup finely sliced pimiento
1 cup plain yogurt

Combine dressing mix with cucumber, green pepper, and pimiento. Fold in yogurt. Cover and chill.

Serve as a dip with raw vegetables.

chili dip

Yield: About 1⅔ cups

⅔ cup low-fat cottage cheese
⅓ cup chili sauce
1 teaspoon chili powder
1½ teaspoons prepared
  horseradish

½ teaspoon salt
⅔ cup plain yogurt

Blend cottage cheese and chili sauce together in a small bowl until fairly smooth. Add chili powder, horseradish, and salt. Fold in yogurt. Cover and chill several hours.

stuffed mushrooms

These mushrooms are perfect for a first course or as a garnish. However, they are too moist to serve as finger food.

Yield: 6 to 8 servings

> 1 pound mushrooms (caps should be 2 to 3 inches in diameter)
> 1 tablespoon melted polyunsaturated margarine (or vegetable oil)
> 3 tablespoons finely chopped onion
> 1 tablespoon water
> 2 tablespoons Madeira
> ¼ cup fine, dry bread crumbs
> ¼ cup grated Parmesan cheese
> ¼ cup low-fat cottage cheese
> 4 tablespoons minced fresh parsley
> ½ teaspoon tarragon
> ¼ teaspoon pepper
> 2 tablespoons melted polyunsaturated margarine

Remove stems from mushrooms. Brush caps with melted margarine (or vegetable oil). Place hollow-side up in a roasting pan. Mince mushroom stems and squeeze in towel to remove moisture.

Cook onion in 1 tablespoon water for 2 to 3 minutes to soften. Add mushroom stems and cook over high heat, stirring frequently, for about 5 minutes or until most of the moisture has disappeared. Add the Madeira and boil it down until it has mostly evaporated. Remove from heat.

Mix in bread crumbs, cheeses, parsley, tarragon, and pepper. Bind together with up to 2 tablespoons melted margarine. Fill mushroom caps with the stuffing. Mushrooms can be prepared ahead to this point. Refrigerate until ready to use.

In a preheated 375°F oven, bake 15 minutes or until the caps are tender and the stuffing is slightly browned.

stuffed pepper slices

stuffed pepper slices

Yield: 4 to 6 servings

1 red pepper
1 green pepper
8 ounces low-fat cottage cheese
2 tablespoons skim milk
1 tablespoon chopped pimiento
1 tablespoon chopped parsley
1 tablespoon chopped watercress
1 tablespoon chopped chives

¼ teaspoon salt
⅛ teaspoon white pepper
1 teaspoon lemon juice
1 envelope (1 tablespoon)
    unflavored gelatin
⅓ cup cold water
Lettuce leaves

Cut off tops of peppers; remove seeds and wash. Cream cottage cheese in the blender. (Thin with milk if necessary.) Remove, and add pimiento, parsley, watercress, chives, salt, pepper, and lemon juice. Soak gelatin in cold water and dissolve completely over simmering water. Add to cheese mixture. Fill peppers with cheese mixture and chill in the refrigerator for at least 2 hours.

Remove and cut each pepper in 4 thick slices. Serve on lettuce leaves.

11

soups

french onion soup

Yield: 4 to 6 servings

3 large onions, thinly sliced
1 tablespoon polyunsaturated
    margarine
1 tablespoon vegetable oil
1 tablespoon flour
6 cups beef broth
2 tablespoons dry white wine or
    vermouth
Salt and pepper to taste
6 slices French bread cut ½ inch
    thick
1 clove garlic, peeled and cut
1 tablespoon cognac
½ cup grated Parmesan cheese

In a covered 4-quart saucepan or Dutch oven, cook onions slowly with margarine and oil for 15 minutes. Stir occasionally. Uncover and increase heat to moderate. Sauté onions, stirring frequently until onions turn golden brown.

Sprinkle onions with flour and stir for 2 to 3 minutes. Blend in hot broth and wine, and adjust seasonings. Simmer partially covered for 1 hour.

Meanwhile place bread slices in a 350°F oven for 30 minutes or until lightly toasted. During baking, rub each slice with the cut garlic clove.

Before serving, add the cognac and divide soup into ovenproof bowls or casseroles. Float rounds of French bread on top of the soup and sprinkle with grated Parmesan cheese.

Bake in a preheated 325°F oven for 15 minutes, until hot, and then set under the broiler for 2 to 3 minutes, until cheese is golden brown. Serve immediately.

cabbage soup

Yield: 6 servings

4 (¼ inch thick) slices Canadian
    bacon, diced
2 onions, sliced
1 turnip, sliced
2 carrots, diced
2 potatoes, cubed
1 small head green cabbage,
    shredded
4 cups chicken stock or bouillon
2 cups water
6 parsley sprigs and bay leaf tied
    together with thread
Salt and pepper to taste
¼ cup grated Parmesan cheese for
    garnish

In a large 6-quart saucepan or pot, combine all ingredients except salt, pepper, and cheese. Simmer partially covered for 1½ to 2 hours. Discard the parsley bundle and season to taste.

Pour into hot soup plates and garnish with cheese.

quick asparagus soup

Yield: 4 servings

1 8-ounce can cut asparagus spears
1 cup chicken broth
Salt and white pepper to taste
Fresh parsley, minced

In a blender, puree the asparagus spears with their liquid and the chicken broth. Heat, adding salt and pepper. Sprinkle with parsley. Serve hot.

fresh tomato soup

fresh tomato soup

Yield: 6 servings

  **6 medium-size tomatoes or about 2
     pounds Italian plum tomatoes
  1 onion, chopped
  1 stalk celery, chopped
  2 cups chicken broth
  1 tablespoon tomato paste
  ½ teaspoon dried basil
  ¼ teaspoon freshly ground pepper
  ½ teaspoon salt
  ½ cup yogurt**

Cut tomatoes into wedges and place in 1½-quart saucepan with all ingredients except yogurt. Simmer uncovered for 30 minutes. Strain to remove tomato skins and seeds. Adjust seasonings. Garnish with spoonfuls of yogurt.

zucchini soup

Yield: 8 servings

  **1 medium onion, chopped
  1 tablespoon polyunsaturated
     margarine
  4 to 6 medium zucchini, sliced
  1 large potato, peeled and diced
  ¼ teaspoon thyme
  ¼ teaspoon rosemary
  ¼ teaspoon basil
  ¼ teaspoon salt
  ⅛ teaspoon pepper
  6 cups chicken broth
  1 cup skim milk**

In a large frypan sauté onion in hot margarine. Add zucchini, potato, herbs, salt, and pepper. After mixture is hot, cook 3 minutes, stirring occasionally. Add chicken broth and simmer for 15 minutes. Puree in blender. Return mixture to saucepan, add milk, and heat slightly. Serve hot or cold.

oriental soup

oriental soup

Yield: 4 to 6 servings

1 quart chicken broth
½ cup bamboo shoots, cut into
    thin strips
2 ounces whole, cooked shrimps
½ pound cooked lean pork, cut
    into thin strips
2 ounces cooked chicken, cut into
    thin strips
½ teaspoon salt
¼ teaspoon soy sauce

Heat the chicken broth and add the remaining ingredients. Simmer for 3 to 4 minutes or until ingredients are hot.

16

chilled spinach soup

Yield: 6 servings

2 cups chicken bouillon
1 10-ounce package frozen chopped spinach
1 cup yogurt

Bring bouillon to a boil in a saucepan. Add frozen spinach and bring to a second boil, breaking spinach apart with a fork. Simmer for 3 minutes. Puree mixture in a blender, a portion at a time. Add yogurt to one portion while blending. Blend the portions together and chill before serving.

andalusian gazpacho

Yield: 4 servings

4 medium tomatoes, peeled and
  chopped
1 small onion, chopped
1 green pepper, seeded and
  chopped
⅛ teaspoon garlic powder
2 tablespoons lemon juice
½ teaspoon salt
Dash freshly ground pepper
Sliced cucumbers for garnish
Chopped onions for garnish
Croutons for garnish

andalusian gazpacho

In a blender, puree tomatoes, onion, and green pepper. Add garlic powder, lemon juice, salt, and pepper.

Serve chilled with garnishes of cucumber slices, chopped onions, and croutons or serve side dishes of finely chopped tomatoes, onions, and green pepper.

17

oxtail soup

Yield: 8 servings

1 2-pound disjointed oxtail or 2
    veal tails
1 medium onion, sliced
2 tablespoons vegetable oil
8 cups water
1 teaspoon salt
4 peppercorns
¼ cup chopped parsley
½ cup diced carrots

1 cup diced celery
1 bay leaf
½ cup tomatoes, drained
1 teaspoon dried thyme
1 tablespoon flour
1 tablespoon polyunsaturated
    margarine
¼ cup Madeira

In a 4-quart Dutch oven, brown oxtail and onion in hot oil for several minutes. Add water, salt, and peppercorns; simmer uncovered for about 5 hours. Add the parsley, carrots, celery, bay leaf, tomatoes, and thyme; continue simmering for 30 minutes longer or until the vegetables are tender.

Strain stock and refrigerate for an hour or more. In a blender, puree the edible meat and vegetables and reserve. Remove fat from top of stock and reheat.

In a large, dry frypan, brown flour over high heat. Cool slightly. Add margarine and blend. Slowly add the stock and vegetables. Correct the seasoning and add Madeira just before serving.

fresh mushroom soup

Yield: 6 servings

1 pound fresh mushrooms
2 tablespoons vegetable oil
2 scallions or shallots, minced
4 cups chicken broth or bouillon

¼ teaspoon salt
½ teaspoon lemon juice
1 lemon, sliced

Wash mushrooms and pat dry with paper towels. Chop very fine or chop small amounts at a time in blender on slowest speed. Heat oil in a frypan and sauté scallions for about 3 minutes or until wilted. Add mushrooms; cook, stirring occasionally, for about 5 minutes. Add broth, salt, and lemon juice. Bring to a boil. Reduce heat to a simmer and cook uncovered for 30 minutes. Blend finished soup in blender or press through a coarse sieve. If sieved, press hard on mushrooms to extract all the liquid. Reheat before serving. Garnish with lemon slices.

white sauce

Yield: Approximately 1 cup

1 tablespoon polyunsaturated
   margarine
1 tablespoon flour
1 cup skim milk
Salt and pepper to taste

Melt the margarine in a small saucepan. Remove from heat and add the flour, stirring with a wire whisk. Add the milk gradually, return to heat, and stir the mixture constantly until the sauce has thickened. Season with salt and pepper.

mornay sauce

Yield: About 1¼ cups

1 tablespoon polyunsaturated
   margarine
1 tablespoon flour
1 cup skim milk
3 tablespoons grated Gruyère
   cheese
1 tablespoon grated Parmesan
   cheese
½ teaspoon Dijon mustard

Melt margarine in a small saucepan. Remove from heat and add the flour, stirring with a wire whisk. Return to a moderate heat. Add the milk gradually, stirring the mixture constantly until the sauce is thickened. Add the remaining ingredients and cook until cheese is melted. Season to taste.

veloute sauce

Yield: Approximately 1 cup

**1 tablespoon polyunsaturated
   margarine**
1 tablespoon flour
**1 cup chicken stock or chicken
   broth**

Melt the margarine in a small saucepan. Remove from the heat and add the flour, stirring with a wire whisk. Add the chicken stock gradually, stirring constantly over a moderate heat.

hollandaise sauce—minceur style

Yield: Approximately 1 cup

**1 tablespoon polyunsaturated
   margarine**
1 tablespoon cornstarch
¾ cup chicken bouillon or broth
**1 egg yolk (or 2 egg whites), lightly
   beaten**
1 tablespoon fresh lemon juice

In a small saucepan, melt margarine and combine with cornstarch. Add the bouillon and cook over medium heat, stirring constantly, until the mixture thickens. Remove from heat.

To prevent the egg yolk from cooking too fast, add 1 tablespoon of the warm sauce to the beaten yolk and mix. Slowly add the egg mixture to the rest of the sauce. Cook over low heat for another minute, stirring constantly. Remove from heat and blend in lemon juice.

mayonnaise—minceur style

Yield: 1¼ cups

1 cup plain yogurt
1 tablespoon Dijon mustard
3 tablespoons vegetable oil
1 tablespoon fresh lemon juice
1 teaspoon minced green onions
2 tablespoons tomato paste
1 tablespoon fresh chopped parsley
**   (or 2 teaspoons dried)**
¼ teaspoon basil
4 drops Tabasco
Salt and pepper to taste

In an electric blender, mix yogurt and mustard. Blend on highest speed. Gradually add oil while blending; then add rest of ingredients. Blend until smooth. Season to taste. This mayonnaise can also be made with a whisk.

lemon sauce—minceur style

Yield: About 1¼ cups

1 lemon, grated and juiced
1 tablespoon cornstarch
1 cup dry white wine
1 tablespoon polyunsaturated
**   margarine**

Blend the lemon juice and cornstarch together. Add wine and mix together until smooth.

In a small saucepan, melt the margarine and add the lemon–wine mixture. Cook and stir until the sauce is slightly thickened and bubbling. Add the grated lemon rind. Serve with fish.

basic sauce variations

basic sauce

    1 pound low-fat cottage cheese
    ½ cup mayonnaise (see recipe for
        mayonnaise—minceur style or
        use imitation mayonnaise)
    6 tablespoons skim milk
    ½ teaspoon salt
    ⅛ teaspoon white pepper
    Juice from half a lemon

Puree cheese in blender. Add the rest of the ingredients and blend for 1 to 2 minutes. Divide the base sauce into five portions and mix with the ingredients listed for individual sauces.

yellow herb sauce

    2 teaspoons prepared mustard
    1 tablespoon chopped chives
    1 teaspoon tarragon
    1 teaspoon chervil
    1 teaspoon chopped parsley

tomato sauce

    1 tablespoon prepared horseradish
    1 teaspoon prepared mustard
    2 tomatoes, peeled and chopped
    1 tablespoon dry white wine

spicy sauce

    1 teaspoon grated lemon rind
    1 tablespoon plain yogurt
    1 teaspoon Worcestershire sauce

paprika sauce

    2 teaspoons paprika
    ½ teaspoon onion powder
    ¼ cup tomato paste
    1 tablespoon tomato catsup
    1 tablespoon dry white wine

mustard–anchovy sauce

    1 teaspoon Chinese mustard (½
        teaspoon dry mustard and ½
        teaspoon vinegar)
    2 anchovy fillets, minced
    1 tablespoon chopped dill

sour-cream substitute
(for a garnish)

1 tablespoon lime or lemon juice
¼ cup skim milk
1 cup low-fat cottage cheese

In a blender, mix ingredients together for 5 seconds.

horseradish cheese sauce
(perfect with roast beef)

Yield: 4 to 6 servings

1 cup low-fat cottage cheese
¼ cup skim milk
2 tablespoons prepared horseradish
2 tablespoons vinegar
1 teaspoon gelatin
¼ cup cold water

Place cheese, milk, horseradish, and vinegar in a blender. Whip for 2 to 3 minutes, until mixture resembles whipped cream. Mix gelatin in water and heat over simmering water to dissolve. Stir gelatin into cheese sauce. Pour into a mold and refrigerate.

creole sauce
(Use with meat, fish or poultry.)

Yield: About 2½ cups

2 tablespoons vegetable oil
2 tablespoons chopped onion
2 tablespoons chopped green pepper
¼ cup sliced mushrooms

2 cups canned tomatoes
½ teaspoon salt
⅛ teaspoon pepper
2 to 3 drops Tabasco sauce
½ teaspoon basil

Heat oil and cook onion, green pepper, and mushrooms over low heat for about 5 minutes. Add tomatoes and seasonings and continue cooking until the sauce is thick, about 40 minutes.

madeira sauce

Yield: 1 cup

¼ pound mushrooms, sliced
2 tablespoons vegetable oil
3 scallions, chopped
1 tablespoon flour
1 cup beef broth or bouillon
½ cup Madeira
Salt and pepper to taste

Sauté mushrooms in hot oil until lightly browned. Remove and reserve. Add scallions and sauté briefly. Sprinkle flour in pan and stir for a minute to cook. Gradually blend in broth. (Use a wire whisk if lumps start to form.) Simmer sauce uncovered for 15 minutes, add Madeira, and simmer again for 5 minutes. Add mushrooms, and season to taste. Delicious on beef or veal.

tomato–wine sauce

Yield: About 1 cup

3 medium tomatoes, peeled and
    cut into pieces (or 1 16-ounce
    can of tomatoes, drained)
1 small onion, chopped
1 bay leaf
½ cup white wine
1 tablespoon polyunsaturated
    margarine
1 tablespoon flour
1 teaspoon sugar
¼ teaspoon oregano
¼ teaspoon basil
1 tablespoon tomato paste
Salt and pepper to taste

In a saucepan, simmer tomatoes, onion, bay leaf, and wine for 30 minutes. Remove the bay leaf and pour the mixture into a blender. Blend for 10 seconds. Melt the margarine, stir in flour, and cook for a minute. Gradually add the tomato puree and stir until thickened. Add the sugar, oregano, basil, and tomato paste. Continue to cook uncovered for 5 to 10 minutes, until flavors have blended and sauce is thick. Season to taste with salt and pepper.

crepe batter—minceur style

Yield: 18 to 22 crepes

3 eggs
1 cup flour
¼ cup instant nonfat dry milk

1 cup water
⅛ teaspoon salt
Vegetable oil for cooking crepes

Combine ingredients and beat with wire whisk or electric blender until smooth. Refrigerate 1 hour or more. It may be necessary to stir batter before cooking to prevent separation.

If a traditional crepe pan is used, place 1 tablespoon of oil in pan and heat until hot. Pour out oil. Pour in 2 to 3 tablespoons crepe batter. Lift pan above heat source and quickly tilt pan in all directions, swirling batter so it covers the bottom of the pan in a very thin layer. Return pan to the heating unit and cook over medium-high heat until the bottom of the crepe is browned. Turn with a spatula and cook other side for a few seconds. Remove from pan and continue with the next crepe. Oil pan only when needed.

Even though this recipe includes whole eggs, each person will consume very little if a standard serving of 2 filled crepes is eaten.

For dessert crepes, add 2 tablespoons of sugar to basic batter.

ham and asparagus crepes

Yield: 6 servings

1 pound fresh asparagus (or
    canned asparagus could be used)
12 crepes
12 thin slices boiled ham
¼ cup grated swiss cheese

Peel the lower third of each asparagus spear and simmer, uncovered, in plenty of lightly salted water for about 15 minutes or until tender. (Omit cooking for canned asparagus.)

Spread out crepes and cover each with a slice of ham. Place 2 or 3 asparagus spears over the ham and roll up the crepes. Place crepes in a lightly greased ovenproof dish. Sprinkle cheese over tops. Bake in a preheated 400°F oven for 15 minutes or until cheese melts.

china crepes

china crepes

Yield: 4 servings

8 ounces lean pork or ham
1 tablespoon water
1 tablespoon dry vermouth
½ teaspoon curry
½ teaspoon paprika
2 scallions, minced
1 green pepper, chopped
1 red pepper, chopped
1 can bean sprouts, drained and heated

8 ounces small shrimps, peeled and deveined
2 tablespoons soy sauce
2 tablespoons white wine, if desired
8 warm crepes
2 tablespoons grated Parmesan cheese
1 tablespoon polyunsaturated margarine

Cut the meat into thin strips. Over high heat, cook meat slightly in water and vermouth. Sprinkle with curry and paprika. Add the scallions and peppers and continue to cook for 2 minutes longer. Add the heated bean sprouts and shrimps. Season with soy sauce, and wine if desired.

Spread the filling on the crepes, roll up, and place seam side down on a greased baking dish. Sprinkle with grated cheese if desired and a few pats of margarine. Bake in a preheated oven at 400°F for 10 to 15 minutes.

ratatouille crepes

Yield: 4 servings

1 onion, finely chopped
1 tablespoon water
1 tablespoon dry vermouth
1 clove garlic, crushed
1 green pepper, chopped
1 zucchini, diced
3 slices of eggplant or 1 small
    eggplant, diced
2 medium tomatoes, peeled,
    seeded, and chopped
½ teaspoon basil
¼ teaspoon oregano
1 teaspoon cornstarch
1 tablespoon water
2 tablespoons tomato sauce
Salt and pepper
8 crepes
Chopped parsley
Pitted black olives
Grated Parmesan cheese

Cook onion in 1 tablespoon of water and the vermouth until translucent. Add the garlic, green pepper, zucchini, and eggplant. Cover, and simmer over a low heat for 15 minutes. Add the tomatoes and herbs, then continue cooking uncovered for another 10 minutes. Drain the vegetables and reserve.

Thoroughly mix 1 teaspoon cornstarch in 1 tablespoon water. Add tomato sauce and cornstarch mixture to the pan juices and heat until sauce thickens. Adjust the seasonings to taste.

Place 2 tablespoons of the ratatouille in each crepe. Roll the crepes and place in a greased ovenproof dish. Bake for 10 minutes in an oven preheated to 400°F.

Pour extra sauce over the crepes. Garnish the dish with chopped parsley and pitted black olives. Sprinkle with a little grated Parmesan cheese and place under the broiler for a minute before serving.

crepes with cashew and chicken filling

Yield: 6 servings

3 tablespoons oil
½ cup cashew nuts, coarsely
  chopped
2 cups uncooked chicken, chopped
½ cup thinly sliced broccoli

1 onion, sliced
1½ cups chicken bouillon
2 tablespoons cornstarch
2 tablespoons soy sauce
12 warm crepes

Heat oil and cook cashews briefly to toast lightly. Remove nuts from pan. In remaining oil, stir in chicken and broccoli; cook about 5 minutes, turning mixture often. Add onion and bouillon. Cover, and simmer for 6 to 8 minutes. Dissolve cornstarch in soy sauce; stir into chicken mixture. Continue stirring over medium heat until thickened. Add cashews. Fill crepes and serve.

black cherry dessert crepes

Yield: 4 servings

2 16-ounce cans pitted black Bing
  cherries
¼ teaspoon ground cinnamon
2 teaspoons sugar
Grated rind and juice of 2 oranges
1 teaspoon arrowroot

1 tablespoon kirsch
8 dessert crepes
1 tablespoon polyunsaturated
  margarine
1 tablespoon confectioner's sugar
Toasted almonds

Drain the cherries and reserve the juice. Simmer the cherries in a covered saucepan over moderate heat with the cinnamon, sugar, and orange rind. (The juice clinging to the cherries will prevent them from burning.) Dissolve the arrowroot in the orange juice and add to the pan of hot cherries. Stir and heat until a thick sauce is formed around the cherries. Add 1 tablespoon kirsch. If sauce appears too thin, add another teaspoon arrowroot dissolved first in 1 tablespoon reserved cherry juice. If the sauce is too thick, thin it out with more juice.

Grease an ovenproof dish. Place 2 tablespoons or more of the cherry filling in each crepe and roll the crepe. Dot the surface of the crepes with margarine and heat in a preheated oven at 400°F for 15 minutes.

Sprinkle the surface of the heated crepes with confectioner's sugar and toasted almonds to garnish.

beef goulash

Yield: 4 servings

1 pound lean beef (round steak)
2 tablespoons vegetable oil
1 large onion, chopped
1 pound potatoes, peeled and cubed
1 green pepper, cut into strips
2 tomatoes, peeled and cut into chunks

1 clove garlic, minced
½ teaspoon caraway seeds
1 3-inch piece of lemon peel, minced
2 teaspoons paprika
½ teaspoon salt
2 cups beef bouillon

Pat meat dry with paper towels and cut into strips approximately ½ inch wide and 2 inches long. Heat oil in a 4-quart Dutch oven: add meat and chopped onion. Cook for 5 minutes or until brown. Add potato cubes and cook for an additional 5 minutes. Add green pepper, tomatoes, garlic, caraway seeds, and lemon peel. Season with paprika and salt. Pour in beef bouillon, cover, and simmer over low heat for 30 minutes. At the end of the cooking time, uncover, and boil the liquid for a few minutes, until the liquid is reduced. Correct the seasoning if necessary.

beef goulash

beef bourguignon

Yield: 4 to 6 servings

3 tablespoons vegetable oil
12 small white onions, peeled
2 pounds lean stewing beef, cubed
1 tablespoon flour
2 cups dry red wine
1 cup beef bouillon
1 clove garlic, minced
1 tablespoon tomato paste

¼ teaspoon thyme
1 bay leaf
½ teaspoon parsley
1 teaspoon salt
½ teaspoon pepper
½ pound fresh mushrooms,
   quartered

Heat oil in a large frypan. Sauté onions lightly and remove from the pan. Add beef cubes and sauté until brown. Sprinkle cubes with flour and toss to coat the meat. Cook for 2 minutes, stirring often. Add wine, bouillon, garlic, tomato paste, and seasonings. Stir well, cover, and simmer slowly for about 3 hours or until meat is tender. Add more bouillon if necessary. The last hour of cooking, add onions. Add mushrooms the last 15 minutes. If sauce is too thin, reduce it by boiling rapidly. Adjust seasoning and serve.

beef stroganoff

Yield: 6 servings

1 pound lean beef (tenderloin,
   sirloin, or round)
½ pound fresh mushrooms, sliced
3 tablespoons oil
1 onion, sliced
1 tablespoon flour

1 cup beef bouillon
2 tablespoons tomato paste
½ teaspoon dry mustard
⅛ teaspoon oregano
2 tablespoons sherry
⅓ cup plain yogurt

Remove fat from meat and slice into thin strips, about 2 inches long. In a heavy frypan, sauté mushrooms in hot oil until tender. Remove and reserve. Sauté onion in the same oil until golden brown. Remove and reserve. Brown meat quickly on all sides until rare. Remove and reserve.

Blend flour into the remaining oil in the frypan and gradually add the bouillon. Stir constantly over low heat until smooth and slightly thickened. Add the tomato paste, dry mustard, oregano, and sherry. Blend well.

Combine the sauce with the meat, mushrooms, and onion in a Dutch oven. Cook for 15 minutes. Blend in the yogurt and heat briefly.

oriental beef and peppers

Yield: 4 to 6 servings

2 green peppers, sliced into rings
3 cups thinly sliced onions
3 green onions, thinly sliced
1 tablespoon water
1 tablespoon dry vermouth
1½ pounds sirloin steak, sliced
    into ⅛-inch slivers
1 clove garlic, crushed

1½ teaspoons sugar
¼ cup sherry
½ teaspoon ginger
¾ cup beef bouillon
3 tablespoons cornstarch blended
    with 2 tablespoons water
½ cup water
2 tablespoons soy sauce

Sauté green peppers, onions, and green onions in water and vermouth until onions are soft. Add beef slivers and cook, stirring over high heat, for 2 minutes. If necessary, add 1 to 2 tablespoons water to keep meat from sticking. Stir in garlic, sugar, sherry, and ginger. Add bouillon and bring mixture to a boil.

In a small bowl, combine cornstarch mixture, water, and soy sauce. Stir into beef mixture and cook until sauce is thickened.

Serve on a bed of hot rice.

stuffed beef rolls

Yield: 6 servings

2 pounds round steak, cut ½ inch
    thick
4 ounces low-fat mozzarella
    cheese, grated
½ cup chopped onion
½ cup chopped celery

¼ cup chopped parsley
2 tablespoons oil
1 cup beef broth or bouillon
    (double strength)
½ teaspoon dry mustard
Salt and pepper to taste

Cut steak into 6 serving pieces; pound to ¼ inch thickness. In a small bowl, combine cheese, onion, celery, and parsley. Divide cheese mixture into two portions. Set aside one portion. Place a small amount of cheese mixture in the center of each piece of steak. Roll each steak and secure it with a toothpick.

Heat oil in a large Dutch oven and brown meat. Drain off excess fat. Combine beef broth and mustard; add to pan with steak rolls. Cover and simmer 45 minutes. Add reserved cheese mixture to Dutch oven; simmer 30 minutes more or until meat is tender. Remove meat to a heated platter. Skim excess fat from pan juices.

Over high heat, reduce sauce by boiling to concentrate flavors, reduce and thicken it. Season to taste. Pour over meat rolls.

beef shreds with carrots and green pepper

Yield: 4 servings

1 tablespoon vegetable oil
2 thin slices of gingerroot
1 clove garlic, cut in half
1 large green pepper, cut into thin
    strips
2 carrots, shredded
1 onion, sliced
1 cup bean sprouts
1 pound cooked beef, thinly sliced
4 water chestnuts, sliced
2 tablespoons soy sauce
1 tablespoon cornstarch in 2
    tablespoons water
½ cup chicken broth

Heat oil in frypan (or wok if available) and quickly brown ginger slices and garlic. Remove and discard the ginger and garlic. Stir-fry the green pepper and carrots for 3 to 4 minutes; remove and reserve. Add the onion to the frypan and stir-fry 2 minutes; reserve with green pepper and carrot mixture. Stir-fry the bean sprouts 1 minute; reserve with other vegetables. Stir-fry the beef strips and water chestnuts until heated. Return the vegetables to the beef in the frypan. Combine the soy sauce, cornstarch mixture, and broth. Add to the beef–vegetable mixture. Heat until the sauce boils and thickens and the ingredients are heated through.

Serve on a plate of hot rice.

beef shreds with carrots and green pepper

swiss steak with vegetable sauce

Yield: 4 servings

1 medium onion, sliced
1 tablespoon vegetable oil
1½ pounds top round steak, cut
    into serving pieces
½ cup beef bouillon
½ cup vegetable juice
⅛ teaspoon thyme
¾ cup sliced carrots
¼ cup chopped celery
1 teaspoon chopped fresh parsley

In a large frypan, cook onion in hot oil until softened. Remove and reserve. Add steak to oil, and brown. Pour bouillon and vegetable juice over steak; add onion and thyme. Cover and simmer slowly for 1 hour. Turn steak over, and cover with carrots and celery. Cook an additional 30 minutes.

When steak is done, remove from vegetables and keep warm. Place vegetables and juices in a blender and puree. Reheat puree if necessary.

Arrange steak on platter, spoon sauce over meat, and sprinkle with parsley. Serve extra sauce separately.

boiled beef

Yield: 6 servings

1 3-pound lean pot roast of beef
    (round or rump)
Water to cover
1 onion, sliced
1 carrot, sliced
5 peppercorns
1 bay leaf
1 can beer

Place all ingredients in a 6-quart saucepan and simmer covered for 3 hours or until meat is tender. Remove meat and strain liquid. Skim off fat and boil liquid to concentrate flavors. Season broth to taste and serve with thin slices of beef.

Delicious with Horseradish Cheese Sauce (see Index).

braised beef with vegetables

Yield: 4 servings

1 red pepper	4 slices round steak, each
1 green pepper	approximately 4 ounces
1 small Spanish onion	½ teaspoon salt
2 medium tomatoes	⅛ teaspoon pepper
2 medium zucchini	⅛ teaspoon dried basil
2 tablespoons vegetable oil	½ cup white wine

Cut peppers in half, remove seeds, and slice into thin strips. Slice onion. Peel tomatoes and cut into eighths. Clean zucchini and cut into ½-inch-thick slices. Heat oil in large frypan or Dutch oven and add all vegetables. Cook for about 10 minutes, stirring occasionally.

Trim fat from round steak. Lightly grease an ovenproof casserole and place ⅓ of vegetable mixture in dish. Arrange round steak on top. Sprinkle with salt, pepper, and basil. Cover with the rest of the vegetables and pour the white wine over the top of the vegetables. Cover casserole and cook in a preheated 350°F oven for 50 minutes. Ten minutes before the end of the cooking time, remove cover so the liquid will be reduced.

braised beef with vegetables

beef en daube

Yield: 6 servings

3 tablespoons vegetable oil
2 pounds beef stew meat
1/2 cup beef bouillon
1 cup dry red wine
1/2 teaspoon salt
1/4 teaspoon dried thyme
1 clove garlic, minced
2 strips orange peel

1 pound small, whole white
onions, peeled
3/4 pound small mushrooms
1 teaspoon sugar
1/2 cup pitted ripe olives
1 10-ounce package frozen peas,
thawed

In a 4-quart Dutch oven, heat 1 tablespoon of the vegetable oil and brown the meat. Pour in bouillon, wine, salt, thyme, garlic, and orange peel. Cover and simmer for 1 hour or until the meat is tender. Cook uncovered for 10 minutes to reduce liquid.

Meanwhile cook the onions in boiling salted water for about 15 minutes or until just tender. Drain. Remove stems from mushrooms, slice, and sauté them with the whole caps in remaining 2 tablespoons vegetable oil. Remove and add to the meat. In the same pan, sauté onions until lightly browned. Sprinkle with sugar and heat to glaze. Add to the meat. Stir in olives and peas, and simmer for 2 minutes. Remove peel. Serve immediately.

beef fillet with summer savory

Yield: 6 servings

2 pounds beef fillet
2 tablespoons vegetable oil
1/2 pound mushrooms, sliced
3 small onions, sliced
1 tablespoon paprika
1/2 cup red wine

1/2 cup beef broth or bouillon
1/2 teaspoon summer savory
1/2 teaspoon salt
1/8 teaspoon pepper
1 tablespoon chopped parsley for
garnish

Slice fillet into thin strips. In a large frypan, heat oil and sauté meat over high heat. Add sliced mushrooms and onions; cook until onions have softened. Stir in the paprika, wine, broth, savory, salt, and pepper. Heat to simmering. Remove meat and raise heat to reduce the sauce quickly. Pour sauce over meat, and garnish with parsley.

beef fillet mexicana

Yield: 4 servings

**1 tablespoon polyunsaturated
    margarine
1 large onion, chopped
1 green pepper, chopped
1 red pepper, chopped
2 tablespoons tomato paste
½ cup hot beef bouillon
½ teaspoon salt
⅛ teaspoon white pepper
Few drops Tabasco sauce
4 servings beef fillet, 4 ounces each
    (or use rib-eye steaks)
¼ to ½ teaspoon freshly ground
    black pepper
2 tablespoons vegetable oil
2 tablespoons tequila (or vodka)
⅛ teaspoon cayenne pepper
¼ teaspoon salt**

Heat margarine in frypan and sauté onion until golden. Add green and red peppers and cook for 2 minutes. Blend tomato paste with hot bouillon and pour over the vegetables. Season with ½ teaspoon of salt, white pepper, and Tabasco sauce. Cover and simmer for 10 minutes.

Meanwhile, pat meat dry with paper towels. Rub generously with coarsely ground black pepper. Heat oil in skillet until very hot and cook meat for 3 minutes on each side. Arrange vegetables on a preheated platter and place steaks on top.

Add tequila or other clear liquor to pan drippings, scraping any particles from the bottom of the pan. Season with cayenne pepper and ¼ teaspoon salt. Pour over the meat and serve immediately.

beef fillet mexicana

38

steak diane

Yield: 4 servings

3 tablespoons chopped scallions
3 tablespoons vegetable oil
3 tablespoons finely chopped
**   chives**
3 tablespoons finely chopped
**   parsley**
1 tablespoon Worcestershire sauce
½ teaspoon salt
¼ teaspoon pepper
4 beef steaks, fillets, or rib-eye
**   steaks**
¼ cup brandy, warmed

Sauté scallions in 1 tablespoon hot vegetable oil for a minute or two. Add the chives, parsley, Worcestershire sauce, salt, and pepper.

In a second frypan, sauté the steaks with the remaining 2 tablespoons hot vegetable oil until done. (Time depends on the thickness of the steak.) Top each steak with some of the scallion mixture. Flame with warmed brandy until the alcohol content is completely burned. Spoon the pan juices over the steaks and serve.

marinated flank steak

Yield: 4 servings

⅔ cup dry red wine
2 tablespoons soy sauce
1 onion, sliced
¼ teaspoon oregano
¼ teaspoon basil

½ teaspoon rosemary
¼ teaspoon thyme
1 thick flank steak (about 1½
**   pounds)**

Mix together the wine, soy sauce, onion, and seasonings. Place the steak in a 13 × 9-inch rectangular glass baking dish and add the marinade. Cover and refrigerate for 24 hours, turning meat at least twice.

Remove steak from the marinade. Broil 4 inches from the heat for about 5 minutes on each side. Cut very thin slices diagonally across the grain. This steak may also be cooked on a charcoal grill for 5 minutes on each side.

stuffed eggplant

Yield: 4 to 6 servings

1 large eggplant
½ cup chopped onion
1 cup chopped mushrooms
1 pound lean ground beef
2 tablespoons vegetable oil
2 tablespoons tomato paste
¼ cup wheat germ
1 teaspoon basil
½ teaspoon chervil
½ teaspoon salt
¼ teaspoon pepper
Parsley for garnish

Cut eggplant in half lengthwise. Remove the pulp, leaving ½ inch of shell. Chop the pulp.

Sauté the onion, mushrooms, and meat in hot oil. Add the tomato paste, wheat germ, seasonings, and eggplant pulp. Cook until the meat is almost done.

Spoon the meat mixture into the eggplant shell and set in a greased ovenproof dish. Bake in a preheated 350°F oven for 30 minutes. Garnish with parsley.

beef patties in red wine

Yield: 4 servings

1 pound lean ground beef
¼ cup finely chopped onion
2 egg whites
¼ cup chopped parsley
½ teaspoon salt
**⅛ teaspoon coarsely ground black
    pepper**

½ cup red wine
¼ pound fresh mushrooms, sliced
**2 tomatoes, peeled and sliced for
    garnish**

Mix meat, onion, egg whites, ½ of the parsley, salt, and pepper. Divide mixture into four patties. Place in a frypan and pour red wine over patties. Cook, covered, at a medium high heat until desired doneness. Remove patties to a preheated platter, add mushrooms to the sauce, and simmer for 3 minutes.

Pour sauce over the patties; garnish with parsley and sliced tomatoes.

tagliatelle bolognese

Yield: 4 servings

1 onion, chopped
1 carrot, diced
1 stalk celery, diced
½ green pepper
2 tablespoons water
1 tablespoon dry vermouth
1 pound lean ground beef
2 8-ounce cans tomato sauce

1 clove garlic, minced
1 bay leaf
1 cup beef bouillon
½ teaspoon salt
¼ teaspoon pepper
¾ pound tagliatelle or other pasta
¼ cup grated Parmesan cheese

In a large frypan, sauté onion, carrot, celery, and green pepper in water and vermouth until the onion turns translucent. Remove the vegetables with a slotted spoon and set aside. Brown the ground beef in the same pan; add more vermouth if necessary to prevent sticking. Drain the ground beef. Add the vegetables, tomato sauce, garlic, bay leaf, bouillon, salt, and pepper. Gently simmer, uncovered, for 30 minutes.

Meanwhile cook pasta according to package directions. When pasta is done to taste, adjust seasonings in sauce and discard the bay leaf.

Turn pasta into a hot serving dish, pour cooked meat sauce into the center, and sprinkle with Parmesan cheese.

herbed meat loaf

Yield: 6 servings

1 pound extra-lean ground beef
½ pound extra-lean ground veal
½ cup bread crumbs
1 small onion, minced
⅛ teaspoon basil
¼ teaspoon oregano

¼ teaspoon summer savory
1 tablespoon vegetable oil
½ teaspoon salt
⅛ teaspoon black pepper
¼ cup skim milk
¼ cup red wine

Mix all ingredients together. Shape into a loaf and place on a baking pan. Bake in a preheated 325°F oven for 1 hour.

picture on opposite page: tagliatelle bolognese

veal cutlets with cherry sauce

Yield: 4 servings

4 lean veal cutlets, about 6 ounces
each
1 tablespoon vegetable oil
½ teaspoon salt
⅛ teaspoon white pepper

¼ cup red wine
2 tablespoons evaporated skimmed
milk
½ pound tart canned cherries
Parsley for garnish

Pat cutlets dry with paper towels. Heat oil in a frypan and brown cutlets on each side for approximately 3 minutes. Season with salt and pepper. Remove cutlets from pan and keep them warm.

Blend red wine and evaporated milk in pan and simmer for 3 minutes. Add drained cherries; heat through and adjust seasonings. Return cutlets to sauce and reheat, but do not boil.

Arrange cutlets on preheated platter, pouring cherry sauce around them. Garnish with parsley.

veal cutlets with cherry sauce

veal with orange slices

Yield: 6 servings

2 oranges
2 teaspoons grated orange rind
12 thinly sliced veal cutlets
2 tablespoons vegetable oil
2 tablespoons brandy, warmed
½ cup beef bouillon
½ teaspoon salt
⅛ teaspoon white pepper
¼ cup orange juice

Grate oranges. Cut away remaining peel on oranges and remove any white membrane. Slice orange into thin rounds. Place in a covered baking pan in a warm oven, 200°F, while preparing the rest of the dish.

In a large frypan, sauté the veal in hot oil until lightly browned. Add the warmed brandy and flame until the alcohol is completely burned off. Stir in the bouillon, salt, pepper, orange juice, and orange rind. Simmer, covered, for 8 minutes. Remove lid and raise heat to reduce sauce for 4 additional minutes.

Serve the veal on a heated serving platter, covered with sauce, and garnish with warm orange slices.

veal with artichokes

Yield: 4 servings

1 clove garlic
1 tablespoon vegetable oil
1 pound veal round, cut into
**   bite-size pieces and pounded**
½ teaspoon salt
⅛ teaspoon pepper
1 cup canned tomatoes
¼ cup sherry
¼ teaspoon oregano
1 10-ounce package frozen
**   artichoke hearts**

In a large frypan, sauté the garlic in hot oil. Remove garlic and discard. Season the veal with salt and pepper. Brown in the oil.

Add the tomatoes, sherry, and oregano; mix well. Add the artichoke hearts; cover and simmer for 1 hour or until the meat is tender.

swiss veal

swiss veal

Yield: 4 servings

1 pound lean veal	½ cup white wine
2 tablespoons vegetable oil	½ teaspoon salt
1 medium onion, chopped	⅛ teaspoon white pepper
½ pound fresh mushrooms	4 tablespoons plain yogurt
1 tablespoon cornstarch	1 teaspoon chopped parsley
½ cup beef bouillon	¼ teaspoon paprika

Cut veal in thin strips crosswise to the grain. Heat oil in a large frypan, add chopped onion, and cook until transparent. Add meat and brown for 5 minutes. Add whole mushrooms or cut them in half if large. Sauté for a minute or two.

Blend cornstarch with a small amount of the bouillon and stir into the meat mixture. Add the rest of the bouillon and the wine. Stir constantly until the mixture bubbles and is thickened. Season with salt and pepper. Gradually blend in yogurt. Heat through, but do not boil.

Arrange on a heated platter; sprinkle with parsley and paprika.

46

veal cutlets swiss style

veal cutlets swiss style

Yield: 4 servings

4 lean veal cutlets, about 6 ounces
   each
2 tablespoons lemon juice
1 small onion
1 clove garlic
2 medium tomatoes
3 tablespoons vegetable oil
1 teaspoon dried parsley (or 1
   tablespoon chopped fresh
   parsley)

½ teaspoon dried basil
½ teaspoon marjoram
¼ cup grated low-fat mozzarella
   cheese
½ teaspoon salt
⅛ teaspoon pepper
2 small dill pickles

Sprinkle cutlets with lemon juice and marinate for 15 minutes. Mince onion and garlic. Peel and chop tomatoes.

Heat 1 tablespoon oil in a frypan. Sauté onion and garlic until golden brown. Add chopped tomato and cook for 5 minutes. Blend in parsley, basil, marjoram, and cheese, stirring constantly. Season with half the amount of salt and pepper. Cover pan and simmer over low heat for 5 minutes.

Heat remaining 2 tablespoons oil in a separate frypan. Pat cutlets dry with paper towels and fry in the oil for approximately 4 minutes on each side. Season with remaining amounts of salt and pepper.

Remove cutlets and arrange on a preheated platter, slightly overlapping. Pour sauce over cutlets. Chop dill pickles very fine and arrange in a strip down the middle of the cutlets.

braised veal rolls

Yield: 6 servings

6 veal chops or slices
1 onion, chopped
4 tablespoons vegetable oil
4 ounces mushrooms, minced
    (about 1 cup)
1 clove garlic, minced
1 cup red wine
1 cup chicken broth

1 tablespoon tomato paste
½ teaspoon salt
⅛ teaspoon pepper
⅛ teaspoon thyme
20 small pitted green olives
8 large fresh mushrooms,
    quartered
2 tablespoons Madeira

Pound veal slices to tenderize and flatten. In a large frypan, sauté onion in 1 tablespoon hot oil for several minutes and add the minced mushrooms. Continue cooking for 5 minutes. Spread the onion–mushroom mixture on each slice of meat. Roll up and tie with string. Brown veal rolls in 2 tablespoons hot oil. Remove and reserve. Drain excess oil.

Add garlic, wine, broth, tomato paste, salt, pepper, and thyme to frypan. Heat to a simmer and add veal rolls. Cover and simmer for 1½ hours.

Meanwhile, place olives in a pan of water and bring to a boil. (This removes some of the salt.) Sauté olives and quartered mushrooms in 1 tablespoon hot oil for 3 to 4 minutes.

When veal is done, remove it from pan and keep it warm. Strain sauce into a clean pan and reduce by boiling to concentrate flavors and thicken it. Add Madeira, olives, and mushrooms. Heat through.

Remove strings from veal rolls. Glaze meat with sauce and garnish with olives and mushrooms.

veal scallopini with tomatoes

Yield: 4 servings

1½ pounds veal, thinly sliced and
    pounded
2 tablespoons vegetable oil
½ pound thinly sliced mushrooms
1 clove garlic, crushed
2 tablespoons chopped parsley

1 tablespoon chopped fresh basil
    or 1 teaspoon dried basil
½ cup peeled, seeded, and diced
    tomatoes
½ cup vermouth
1 tablespoon Parmesan cheese

In Dutch oven, sauté veal in hot oil until brown. Add remaining ingredients. Cover and cook in a preheated 350°F oven for 40 minutes.

veal marengo

Yield: 4 servings

1 pound veal (lean breast or lean
  stew meat)
2 tablespoons vegetable oil
1 medium onion, chopped
¼ pound fresh mushrooms, sliced
1 medium carrot, sliced
1 tablespoon tomato paste
½ teaspoon salt
⅛ teaspoon pepper

1 bay leaf
1 teaspoon dried thyme
½ cup hot water
½ cup white wine
¼ cup plain yogurt
1 tablespoon sliced truffles for
  garnish (optional)
1 tomato for garnish
Parsley for garnish

Cube veal. In a large frypan, brown meat in hot oil for several minutes. Remove meat and keep it warm. Add chopped onion, mushrooms, and carrot to pan drippings; cook for 5 minutes. Stir in tomato paste. Season with salt and pepper; add the bay leaf and thyme. Pour in water and wine and return browned meat to pan. Cover and simmer for about 30 minutes. Cool slightly, and gradually add the yogurt. Reheat over low heat, if necessary, but do not simmer. Remove the bay leaf and adjust seasonings.

Serve veal on a preheated platter, garnished with sliced truffles, tomato sections, and parsley.

veal marengo

goulash soup

Yield: 6 servings

3 medium onions, sliced
1 clove garlic, finely chopped
3 tablespoons vegetable oil
2 teaspoons paprika
½ pound lean veal, ground
½ pound lean pork, ground

3 cups beef stock or bouillon
½ teaspoon salt
⅛ teaspoon pepper
2 medium potatoes, sliced
3 small tomatoes, chopped

In a 4-quart Dutch oven, sauté onions and garlic in hot oil until lightly browned. Add paprika and cook for 1 minute. Stir in ground meats and sauté until lightly browned. Gradually add the stock and seasonings. Cover and simmer for 10 minutes. Add the potatoes and tomatoes. Cover and simmer for 20 minutes or until the potatoes are soft.

veal cutlets with capers

veal cutlets with capers

Yield: 4 servings

4 lean veal cutlets, about 6 ounces each	**½ small jar capers**
2 tablespoons lemon juice	**¼ cup dry white wine**
½ teaspoon salt	**1 bay leaf**
⅛ teaspoon pepper	**3 tablespoons evaporated skim milk**
½ teaspoon paprika	**Sliced pickled beets for garnish**
1 tablespoon vegetable oil	**4 lettuce leaves for garnish**

Sprinkle cutlets with lemon juice and season with salt, pepper, and paprika. Heat oil in a frypan and fry cutlets for 3 minutes on the first side. Turn cutlets over and add drained capers to pan. Fry again for 3 minutes; remove cutlets and arrange on a preheated platter.

Pour wine into the pan, scraping loose any brown particles from the bottom of the frypan. Add bay leaf and simmer liquid for 3 minutes. Remove bay leaf. Blend in evaporated milk and adjust seasonings.

Pour sauce over cutlets. Cut beets into strips and arrange on lettuce leaves as a garnish.

51

veal stew continental

Yield: 4 servings

1 tablespoon vegetable oil
2 teaspoons soy sauce
1 pound lean veal stew meat, cut in
    1-inch cubes
1 large onion, chopped
¾ cup water or tomato juice
¼ teaspoon pepper

½ teaspoon salt
1 clove garlic, minced (optional)
1 teaspoon rosemary
2 small carrots, sliced thin
2 large green peppers, sliced thin
½ pound fresh mushrooms, sliced
½ teaspoon grated lemon rind

Heat oil and soy sauce in a large frypan. Sauté veal and onion until brown. Add water or tomato juice, pepper, salt, garlic (if desired), and rosemary. Cover and simmer for 45 minutes. Check occasionally and add more water if needed.

Add carrots, green peppers, and mushrooms. Continue cooking for 30 to 40 minutes or until veal is tender and vegetables are done. Add extra water if necessary. Garnish with lemon rind.

veal stufino

Yield: 4 servings

1 pound veal shoulder, cut in
    chunks
1 tablespoon vegetable oil
1 carrot, finely chopped
1 stalk celery, finely chopped
1 onion, finely chopped
1 clove garlic, minced
½ cup dry white wine
2 tomatoes, peeled and chopped
½ teaspoon salt
¼ teaspoon pepper

In a large frypan, sauté veal in hot oil. Add carrot, celery, onion, garlic, and wine. Stir and scrape particles from bottom of pan. Simmer for 5 minutes.

Add tomatoes, salt, and pepper. Cover and simmer over low heat for 1½ hours. Uncover, raise heat, and reduce the sauce just before serving.

vegetable stew with lamb

Yield: 6 servings

2 tablespoons vegetable oil
1 pound lean lamb, cut in bite-size pieces
1 medium onion, chopped
1 small head cabbage, shredded
1 stalk celery, sliced
2 medium carrots, sliced
1 stalk leek, sliced
6 cups hot beef bouillon

2 medium potatoes, cubed
1 small head of cauliflower, separated into florets
1 10-ounce package frozen green beans
2 tablespoons tomato paste
½ teaspoon salt
¼ teaspoon white pepper
Parsley to garnish

Heat oil in a 4-quart Dutch oven or saucepan. Brown meat for about 5 minutes. Add onion, and sauté until golden brown. Add cabbage, celery, carrots, leek, and hot bouillon. Bring to a boil and simmer for 1 hour.

Add potatoes, cauliflower, and beans. Continue simmering for 20 to 30 minutes, until the vegetables are tender. Thin tomato paste with a little broth, and add to the stew. Season with salt and pepper. Garnish with chopped parsley.

vegetable stew with lamb

lamb stew

lamb stew

Yield: 4 servings

1 tablespoon vegetable oil
1 pound boneless lamb, cut in
    1-inch cubes
1 tablespoon flour
1 teaspoon salt
¼ teaspoon pepper
1 cup white wine
1 tablespoon tomato paste
2 cups water

1 clove garlic, minced
½ pound carrots, cubed
2 turnips, cubed
¼ pound fresh green beans,
    trimmed
6 small potatoes, peeled and
    quartered
6 small whole onions, peeled
¼ pound fresh green peas

Heat oil in a 2-quart saucepan. Brown lamb well on all sides. Sprinkle with flour, salt, and pepper; stir well to coat lamb. Add wine, tomato paste, water, and garlic. Bring to a simmer, cover, and cook 40 minutes. Add all vegetables except peas. Cover, and cook slowly about 30 minutes, until lamb is tender and vegetables are done. Add peas and cook 8 minutes or until done.

54

curry lamb ragout

curry lamb ragout

Yield: 4 servings

1 pound lean lamb meat	⅛ teaspoon white pepper
2 tablespoons vegetable oil	1 green pepper, cut in strips
½ teaspoon sage	1 8-ounce can sliced mushrooms
Grated rind of half a lemon	2 tomatoes, peeled and quartered
1 medium onion, chopped	1 tart apple, peeled, cored, and
2 cups beef bouillon	coarsely chopped
1 tablespoon curry powder	½ cup plain yogurt
½ teaspoon salt	

Cut meat into 1-inch cubes. Heat oil in a heavy saucepan or Dutch oven. Add meat, sage, and lemon rind; brown meat on all sides. Add onion, and sauté lightly. Drain off excess oil. Stir in bouillon, cover saucepan, and simmer for 50 minutes.

Season with curry, salt, and pepper. Add sliced green pepper and simmer uncovered for 5 minutes. Stir in drained mushrooms, tomatoes, and apple. Simmer for another 5 minutes. Cool mixture slightly and gradually add yogurt to ragout. Heat thoroughly without boiling. Serve at once.

baked kibbek

Yield: 6 servings

1 cup crushed bulgar wheat
(sold at specialty food
stores)
¼ cup chopped pine nuts
1 tablespoon vegetable oil
2 pounds lean ground lamb
1 small onion, minced
1 teaspoon salt

⅛ teaspoon black pepper
½ teaspoon cinnamon
½ cup water
1 tablespoon polyunsaturated
margarine
Yogurt to accompany dish if
desired

Rinse the crushed wheat, drain, and set aside for a few minutes. Meanwhile, brown the nuts in a frypan with hot oil. Mix together the ground meat, onion, salt, pepper, cinnamon, and water.

Spread half the meat mixture in a greased baking pan and sprinkle with toasted nuts. Spread the remaining meat mixture in a top layer. Cut mixture in squares. Dot with margarine, and bake at 350°F for 30 minutes. Serve with a side dish of yogurt if desired.

pork chops with ham

Yield: 4 servings

2 tablespoons lemon juice
4 lean pork chops
4 ounces lean cooked ham
2 dill pickles
2 tablespoons vegetable oil

1 8-ounce container plain yogurt
1 tablespoon capers
½ teaspoon salt
⅛ teaspoon pepper
Parsley for garnish

Sprinkle lemon juice on the pork chops and set aside. Cut ham into julienne strips. Cut dill pickles in half lengthwise, remove seeds with a teaspoon, and chop.

Heat oil in a large, heavy frypan. Pat chops with paper towels to remove excess moisture. Place chops in frypan and thoroughly brown both sides. Add ham and chopped dill pickles and cook for 5 minutes. Stir in yogurt and capers. Add salt and pepper. Continue cooking uncovered over low heat for an additional 5 minutes to blend flavors.

Arrange chops on a preheated platter, pour sauce over, and garnish with parsley.

pork chops with ham

pork and vegetable casserole

Yield: 4 servings

2 tablespoons vegetable oil
1 pound lean pork, cut into
    bite-size pieces
1 medium onion, chopped
2 pounds green cabbage, finely
    shredded
3 medium potatoes, peeled and cut
    into 1-inch cubes

1½ cups hot beef bouillon
½ teaspoon salt
⅛ teaspoon pepper
½ teaspoon caraway seeds
1 sprig of parsley, chopped

Heat oil in a large Dutch oven. Add meat cubes, and brown on all sides for about 10 minutes. Add the onion, and sauté lightly. Stir in the cabbage and potatoes. Add bouillon, and season with salt, pepper, and caraway seeds. Cover, and simmer for 50 minutes. Correct seasonings if necessary. Serve garnished with chopped parsley.

pork and vegetable casserole

pork loin with cider and apples

Yield: 6 servings

> **2 pounds pork loin (have butcher remove bone)**
> **2 tablespoons vegetable oil**
> **1 small onion, chopped**
> **2 cooking apples, peeled, cored, and sliced**
> **1 cup cider**
> **½ cup chicken broth or bouillon**
> **½ teaspoon salt**
> **¼ teaspoon pepper**
> **1 tablespoon cornstarch**
> **1 tablespoon apple brandy**

Cut the pork loin into ½-inch slices and brown on both sides in hot oil. Remove pork and add the onion and the apple slices. Sauté for 3 minutes and again add the pork. Stir in the cider, broth, and seasonings. Simmer for 30 minutes or until the pork is tender. Dissolve cornstarch in apple brandy and stir into sauce until mixture bubbles and thickens. Adjust seasoning.

Serve with wild rice and red cabbage.

pork with apples

Yield: 6 servings

> **2 pounds boneless pork loin, cut in 1½-inch cubes**
> **2 tablespoons vegetable oil**
> **4 leeks or 2 onions, sliced**
> **2 green cooking apples, peeled, cored, and sliced**
> **1 teaspoon cumin**
> **1 tablespoon flour**
> **1¼ cups apple cider or apple juice**
> **¼ cup dry vermouth**
> **½ teaspoon salt**
> **⅛ teaspoon freshly ground black pepper**

Brown the pork cubes in hot oil, remove from pan, and reserve. Cook the leeks or onions and apples in the same oil for 5 minutes, until softened. Stir in the cumin and flour, and cook 1 minute. Transfer apple mixture to a casserole. Add pork and rest of ingredients. Cover and cook at 350°F for 1 hour.

pork chops braised in tomatoes with garlic sauce

Yield: 6 servings

6 lean loin pork chops, 1 inch thick
3 tablespoons vegetable oil
1 clove garlic, minced
½ teaspoon dried oregano
¼ teaspoon dried thyme
1 bay leaf
½ teaspoon salt
½ cup dry red wine
1 cup tomato sauce
1 tablespoon tomato paste
½ pound green peppers, cut in
   strips
½ pound fresh mushrooms,
   quartered

Trim fat from pork chops. In a large frypan, heat 2 tablespoons of the oil, and sauté chops for 2 to 3 minutes on each side or until brown. Remove and reserve chops.

Pour off excess oil. Add garlic, oregano, thyme, bay leaf, and salt; cook and stir for 30 seconds. Add the wine and boil to reduce it to ¼ cup, scraping particles from bottom of pan.

Stir in the tomato sauce and tomato paste and return the chops to the frypan. Baste chops with sauce; cover, and simmer for 50 minutes. Baste occasionally.

Meanwhile heat the remaining 1 tablespoon oil in another frypan. Stir-fry the green peppers for about 3 to 4 minutes. Add the mushrooms and stir-fry for 1 to 2 minutes. Transfer green peppers and mushrooms to pan with chops. Cover, and simmer for 5 minutes. Uncover pan and continue to simmer for a few minutes longer, until the meat is tender and the sauce is reduced.

Arrange the chops on a heated platter and spoon the vegetables and sauce over them.

marinated rabbit

Yield: 6 servings

1 3-pound rabbit
1 teaspoon salt
¼ teaspoon pepper
3 tablespoons vegetable oil

marinade

2 cups red wine
2 cups chicken broth
1 teaspoon allspice
2 bay leaves
1 teaspoon thyme

sauce

1 dozen pickled white onions
  (cocktail size)
1 dozen stuffed green olives, sliced
½ pound fresh mushrooms, sliced
2 tablespoons polyunsaturated
  margarine

Cut rabbit into serving pieces. Rub with salt and pepper, and put in large bowl. Add the marinade, and refrigerate overnight.

Drain the pieces of rabbit, but do not pat dry. Strain and reserve the marinade. In a large frypan over high heat, quickly brown all sides of the rabbit pieces in hot vegetable oil. When brown, pour in reserved marinade and simmer over low heat for 1 hour or until rabbit is tender.

Just before rabbit is done, sauté onions, olives, and mushrooms in hot margarine. Add to rabbit mixture. Serve with boiled potatoes.

61

poultry

chicken cacciatore

Yield: 4 servings

1 3-pound chicken
3 tablespoons vegetable oil
1 clove garlic
½ teaspoon salt
¼ teaspoon pepper
1 teaspoon rosemary

6 anchovy fillets, chopped
⅓ cup wine vinegar
1⅓ cups dry red wine
3 tablespoons tomato paste
½ cup chicken bouillon

Cut chicken into serving pieces. In a large frypan, heat oil and sauté chicken and garlic for 5 minutes. Turn chicken often. Remove garlic. Add salt, pepper, rosemary, anchovies, wine vinegar, and red wine. Simmer, uncovered, until the liquid is reduced by one-third. Dissolve tomato paste in chicken bouillon and pour over the chicken. Simmer, covered, for 20 minutes or until the chicken is done.

chicken salad with asparagus

Yield: 6 servings

1 3-pound chicken
½ teaspoon salt
⅛ teaspoon pepper
¼ teaspoon paprika
1 16-ounce can peas, drained
1 14½-ounce can asparagus pieces, drained

1 8-ounce can sliced mushrooms, drained
1 8-ounce container plain yogurt
2 tablespoons mayonnaise
1 teaspoon dillweed
½ teaspoon salt
⅛ teaspoon pepper

Place chicken in center of a large square of aluminum foil. Sprinkle with salt, pepper, and paprika. Wrap, and cook in a preheated 350°F oven for 1 hour. Cool, and remove meat from bone. Cut into bite-size pieces.

In a large bowl, add chicken, peas, asparagus, and mushrooms. Mix together the yogurt, mayonnaise, dillweed, salt, and pepper and gently combine with other ingredients. Marinate in the refrigerator for 2 hours before serving.

broiled chicken with mushrooms

Yield: 4 servings

   1 3-pound chicken
   3 tablespoons polyunsaturated
       margarine, melted
   2 onions, cut into quarters
   2 tablespoons polyunsaturated
       margarine
   ½ pound mushrooms, stemmed
   1 teaspoon salt
   ½ teaspoon pepper
   2 tablespoons cognac

Split chicken in half and brush with 3 tablespoons melted margarine. Broil 5 inches from heat for about 20 minutes. Brush with margarine every 5 minutes. Do not allow the skin to burn or blister.

Meanwhile sauté onions for 5 minutes in 2 tablespoons margarine. Add mushrooms and cook another 5 minutes. Season with salt and pepper. Pour cognac over vegetables and set ablaze.

When chicken is cooked, split each piece in two. Arrange vegetables on platter with chicken.

chicken italian

Yield: 4 servings

   2 tablespoons vegetable oil
   1 chicken (3 pounds), cut into
       serving pieces and skin removed
   ½ teaspoon salt
   ⅛ teaspoon pepper
   1 large green pepper, sliced
   4 small white onions, peeled
   1 clove garlic, minced
   1 cup canned tomatoes
   1 cup sliced mushrooms

Heat oil in a large frypan and brown chicken on all sides for about 10 minutes. Add all ingredients except mushrooms to pan. Cover and simmer slowly for 40 minutes. Add mushrooms and simmer for 20 minutes or until the mushrooms and chicken are tender.

oriental chicken with chinese mushrooms

(served over Oriental vegetables)

Yield: 4 servings

2 tablespoons soy sauce
1 tablespoon cornstarch
1 small fryer chicken, boned,
skinned, and cut into bite-size
pieces
1 tablespoon vegetable oil
1 clove garlic, cut in half
lengthwise
3 slices gingerroot, ⅛-inch thick
½ pound fresh mushrooms,
quartered
4 dried black Chinese mushrooms
(soaked in warm water for 30
minutes, drained, and diced)
2 tablespoons hoisin sauce (found
in Oriental food stores)

Combine soy sauce and cornstarch; pour over chicken, and marinate ½ hour. In the hot oil, brown the garlic and ginger slices for 2 to 3 minutes. Remove and discard the garlic and ginger. Add the two types of mushrooms to the pan and stir-fry for 1 to 2 minutes. Remove mushrooms and reserve. Stir-fry the chicken 3 to 4 minutes or until done. Add the hoisin sauce and return mushrooms to pan. Heat through and serve over Oriental Vegetables (see Index).

picture on opposite page: oriental chicken with chinese mushrooms served over oriental vegetables

chicken in curry and wine sauce

Yield: 6 servings

1 cup chicken broth
½ cup dry white wine
1 clove garlic, minced
1 teaspoon curry powder
½ teaspoon seasoned salt
¼ teaspoon pepper
3 chicken breasts, split
1 tablespoon cornstarch
2 tablespoons cold water
1 3-ounce can sliced mushrooms,
**   drained**
Paprika or parsley for garnish

In a large frypan, combine broth, wine, garlic, curry, salt, and pepper; bring to a boil. Add chicken; reduce heat. Cover; simmer 25 to 30 minutes or until chicken is tender. Remove chicken to a warm platter.

Blend cornstarch and water; slowly stir into pan juices. Cook and stir over low heat until sauce bubbles. Stir in the mushrooms and continue heating for 1 to 2 minutes.

Pour sauce over chicken. Garnish with paprika and parsley as desired.

marinated chicken with sesame seeds

Yield: 4 servings

½ cup soy sauce
1 tablespoon sugar
2 thin slices fresh ginger
1 3-pound chicken, cut into serving
**   pieces**
2 tablespoons vegetable oil
2 tablespoons sesame seeds,
**   toasted**

Mix marinade: soy sauce, sugar, and ginger. Marinate chicken in a shallow baking dish for 2 hours. Turn once. Broil over charcoal or in the oven for about 30 minutes; baste often with marinade and oil.

Sprinkle with sesame seeds and serve.

spicy roast chicken

Yield: 4 servings

    1 cup plain yogurt
    3 cloves garlic, crushed
    2 teaspoons fresh ginger, grated
    ⅓ cup lime juice
    1 tablespoon coriander, ground
    1 teaspoon cumin
    ½ teaspoon cayenne pepper
    1 whole chicken (3 pounds)
    Lime wedges
    1 onion, sliced and steamed

Mix yogurt, garlic, ginger, lime juice, and spices. Rub chicken inside and out with yogurt mixture. Place chicken in a bowl and pour the rest of the marinade over. Cover, and refrigerate for 24 hours. Turn chicken at least once.

Remove chicken from marinade and roast in a preheated 375°F oven for 1 hour or until done. Baste with marinade during cooking.

Disjoint and serve with wedges of lime and onion slices.

tomatoes stuffed with chicken

Yield: 6 servings

    ½ teaspoon salt
    ¼ teaspoon tarragon
    1 cup plain yogurt
    1 can (8 ounces) crushed pineapple,
        drained
    1½ cups diced, cooked chicken
    ½ cup toasted slivered almonds
    1 stalk celery, finely diced
    6 tomatoes

To prepare dressing, stir salt and tarragon into yogurt. Chill.

In a separate bowl combine pineapple, chicken, almonds, and celery. Chill.

Just before serving, stir dressing lightly into chicken mixture.

Cut tomatoes partially into sections and fill with salad. Garnish with parsley, if desired.

chicken with green peppers and bamboo shoots in oyster sauce

Yield: 4 servings

sauce

1 small onion, sliced

1 tablespoon soy sauce

2 tablespoons oyster sauce (found in Oriental food stores and some supermarkets)

¾ cup chicken broth

2 1 teaspoon brown sugar

1 teaspoon freshly grated gingerroot

1 tablespoon cornstarch in 2 tablespoons water

chicken–vegetable mixture

1 tablespoon vegetable oil

1 large green pepper, cut into ¾-inch cubes

¼ cup sliced bamboo shoots

¼ pound small whole mushrooms

2 whole chicken breasts, split, skinned, boned, and cut into pieces

½ cucumber, peeled and cut into chunks

chicken with green peppers and bamboo shoots in oyster sauce

To make the sauce, simmer together all sauce ingredients for 8 to 10 minutes. Stir occasionally.

Meanwhile heat oil in frypan (or wok if available) and stir-fry the green pepper for 3 minutes. Remove and reserve. Stir-fry the bamboo shoots and mushrooms for 2 to 3 minutes. Reserve with the green pepper. Add the chicken to the frypan and stir-fry 3 to 4 minutes or until done. Return the vegetables to the pan with the chicken. Add the cucumber.

Immediately add the oyster sauce and heat through. Serve with rice.

sweet-and-sour chicken with vegetables and fruit

Yield: 4 servings

2 tablespoons soy sauce
1 tablespoon cornstarch
2 whole chicken breasts, halved, skinned, boned, and cut into bite-size cubes
1 tablespoon vegetable oil
1 cucumber scored lengthwise with tines of a fork and cut into bite-size cubes
½ cantaloupe, seeded, rinded, and cut into bite-size pieces

1 sweet red pepper (or green pepper), cubed
3 ounces blanched, whole almonds

sauce

2 tablespoons brown sugar
2 tablespoons vinegar
½ cup pineapple juice (unsweetened)
1 tablespoon cornstarch in 2 tablespoons cold water

Combine soy sauce and cornstarch. Coat chicken pieces thoroughly. Heat oil in a large frypan (or wok if available) and stir-fry the chicken pieces for 3 to 4 minutes. Add the cucumber, cantaloupe, and pepper.

Mix together the ingredients for the sweet-and-sour sauce and add to the chicken mixture. Heat, stirring often, until the sauce boils and the ingredients are heated through. Add the almonds. Serve at once.

chicken mandarin

Yield: 4 servings

1 tablespoon Madeira wine
2 tablespoons raisins
1 chicken, approximately 2½
    pounds
½ teaspoon salt
1 teaspoon paprika
⅛ teaspoon pepper
2 tablespoons vegetable oil
1 11-ounce can mandarin oranges
½ cup chicken bouillon
1 clove garlic, minced
1 ounce sliced almonds
1 tablespoon cornstarch
¼ cup water
1 tablespoon soy sauce
½ teaspoon ground ginger
2 tablespoons plain yogurt

Sprinkle Madeira wine over the raisins; cover, and let soak. Cut cleaned chicken into 4 pieces. Mix salt, paprika, and pepper, then rub chicken pieces with this mixture. Heat oil in a large, heavy frypan and brown chicken on all sides, approximately 10 minutes.

Drain mandarin oranges; reserve juice. Pour juice in measuring cup and add enough bouillon to make 1 cup of liquid. Pour over chicken. Add minced garlic; cover frypan, and simmer chicken for 30 minutes.

Meanwhile toast the almonds by placing them on a baking sheet in a 300°F oven and turning frequently until lightly browned. Reserve.

Stir the soaked raisins and liquid into the chicken mixture and continue simmering for another 5 minutes. Remove the chicken pieces and arrange on a preheated platter.

Blend the cornstarch with a small amount (¼ cup) of water and stir into the sauce. Cook until the sauce is thickened. Season with soy sauce and ginger. Add drained oranges and heat through but do not boil. Gradually stir in the yogurt.

Pour sauce over the chicken pieces and sprinkle the toasted almonds over the top.

picture on opposite page: sweet-and-sour chicken with vegetables and fruit

picture on next pages: chicken mandarin

chicken paprika

Yield: 4 servings

1 chicken, 2½ to 3 pounds	1 small carrot, sliced
1 tablespoon vegetable oil	1 small stalk celery, sliced
1 large onion, chopped	2 medium potatoes, peeled and
2 tablespoons paprika	cubed
1 clove garlic, minced	½ cup chicken broth or bouillon
½ teaspoon salt	3 tomatoes
1 teaspoon caraway seeds	1 red pepper, cubed
1 cup hot water	1 green pepper, cubed
1 scallion or leek, cut lengthwise	Parsley for garnish
and sliced	

Skin and bone chicken; cut into bite-size pieces.

Heat oil in a 4-quart Dutch oven and sauté onion. Sprinkle 1 tablespoon of the paprika over onions and stir well. Add minced garlic, salt, caraway seeds, and ½ cup of the hot water. Simmer over low heat for 10 minutes. Add chicken pieces. Cover, and simmer for 5 minutes. Add additional ½ cup of water; cover, and simmer for 15 minutes. Add scallion, carrot, celery, potatoes, and ½ cup chicken broth to chicken. Simmer again for 10 minutes.

Peel and chop 2 tomatoes. Add peppers, the 2 chopped tomatoes, and the remaining 1 tablespoon of paprika. Cover, and continue simmering for another 15 minutes. Correct seasoning if necessary.

Serve garnished with 1 sliced tomato and chopped parsley.

baked spiced chicken

Yield: 4 servings

1 cup plain yogurt
1¼ teaspoons salt
1 small clove garlic, crushed
½ teaspoon ground cardamom
½ teaspoon chili powder

¼ teaspoon cinnamon
¼ teaspoon ginger
1 chicken (2½ to 3 pounds),
    quartered

Combine yogurt, salt, garlic, and spices. Place chicken in shallow dish; pour yogurt mixture over chicken, and marinate overnight.

Place chicken skin side up in baking pan. Spoon half of the marinade over chicken. Bake 1¼ to 1½ hours, until tender, in preheated 350°F oven. Baste occasionally.

To serve, spoon hot marinade over chicken.

chicken in white wine and cognac

Yield: 6 servings

3 chicken breasts, split and
    skinned
2 tablespoons vegetable oil
¼ pound boiled ham
4 carrots, peeled and cut in chunks
12 small white boiling onions,
    peeled
1 clove garlic
¼ teaspoon thyme
1 bay leaf
3 sprigs parsley

¼ teaspoon tarragon
1 tablespoon tomato paste
½ cup chicken broth
1½ cups white wine
½ teaspoon salt
¼ teaspoon pepper
1 tablespoon flour
1 tablespoon polyunsaturated
    margarine
2 tablespoons cognac

In a 4-quart Dutch oven, brown chicken pieces in hot oil. When brown, drain off excess oil.

Cut ham into ¼-inch strips. Add ham and vegetables to the browned chicken. Add rest of ingredients except flour, margarine, and cognac. Simmer for 1 hour; remove parsley sprigs and bay leaf.

Cream flour with margarine to blend. Add to mixture and stir until lightly thickened.

Float cognac over the top, light with match, and serve.

chicken provençale

chicken provençale

Yield: 4 servings

**4 whole chicken breasts, each
approximately 8 to 10 ounces
3 tablespoons vegetable oil
½ teaspoon salt
⅛ teaspoon white pepper
1 medium tomato
5 black olives
1 clove garlic, minced
½ cup dry white wine
3 tablespoons water
¼ teaspoon instant chicken
bouillon (or ½ cube)
¼ cup yogurt
Parsley for garnish**

Bone chicken breasts.

Heat oil in a large frypan and fry chicken breasts, approximately 15 minutes, until they are golden brown and completely cooked. Season with salt and pepper. Arrange on a preheated platter and keep warm.

Peel and chop tomato; slice olives. Add tomato, olives, and minced garlic to pan drippings. Pour in wine and water; stir in dry bouillon. Bring to a boil and simmer uncovered for 8 minutes. Cool sauce slightly, and gradually add yogurt. Warm sauce over low heat if necessary.

Pour sauce over chicken breasts; garnish with parsley.

chicken in yogurt and wine sauce

Yield: 8 servings

4 large whole chicken breasts, split
    and skin removed
2 tablespoons polyunsaturated
    margarine
2 tablespoons flour
½ cup chicken bouillon

½ cup yogurt
2 tablespoons white wine
1 teaspoon grated lemon rind
½ teaspoon salt
⅛ teaspoon pepper
½ cup sliced mushrooms

Melt 1 tablespoon of margarine in a large, shallow baking pan, and arrange chicken breasts in the pan. Bake in a preheated 350°F oven for about 30 minutes.

Meanwhile melt remaining 1 tablespoon margarine in a saucepan and stir in flour. Cook for 1 to 2 minutes. Stir in bouillon and cook until mixture is thickened. Blend in yogurt, wine, lemon rind, salt, and pepper.

Turn chicken breasts. Cover with sliced mushrooms and pour sauce over tops. Bake, uncovered, for 20 minutes or until tender. Place under a broiler for about 2 minutes to brown top.

chicken kiev with sherry sauce

Yield: 4 servings

2 whole chicken breasts, split,
    boned, and skinned
1 tablespoon chopped chives
1 tablespoon chopped parsley
½ clove garlic, minced
¼ teaspoon salt
⅛ teaspoon pepper

½ cup low-fat mozzarella cheese,
    grated
Toothpicks
2 tablespoons vegetable oil
1 tablespoon flour
¼ cup dry sherry
1 cup chicken bouillon or broth

Pound each chicken breast half with the flat side of a meat mallet to ¼ inch thickness. Sprinkle seasonings evenly over chicken pieces. Cover surfaces with grated cheese and roll up each half breast with cheese enclosed. Secure with a toothpick.

Heat oil in a large frypan and sauté chicken rolls until golden brown, about 8 minutes. Place in shallow baking dish. Preheat oven to 350°F.

To make the sauce, stir flour into drippings in frypan; stir until smooth. Remove from heat. Add sherry and bouillon to drippings. Return to heat and heat to boiling, stirring constantly. Reduce sauce by boiling until slightly thickened. Spoon over chicken; cover. Bake 30 minutes. Remove toothpicks before serving.

chicken soufflé

Yield: 4 servings

1½-quart soufflé mold (or
    casserole with straight sides)
⅓ cup grated skim-milk
    mozzarella cheese
2 tablespoons polyunsaturated
    margarine
2 tablespoons flour

½ cup skim milk, heated
¼ teaspoon salt
⅛ teaspoon pepper
⅛ teaspoon nutmeg
6 egg whites (¾ cup)
¼ teaspoon salt
⅔ cup cooked chicken, cubed

Preheat oven to 400°F. Grease soufflé mold and sprinkle insides with 1 tablespoon of the grated cheese.

Melt margarine, add flour, and cook together over low heat for 2 minutes. Remove from heat; add warm milk and seasonings. Return to heat and boil for 1 minute, stirring constantly. Again remove from heat.

Beat the egg whites and salt until stiff peaks are formed. Stir one-third of whites into milk mixture. Fold in chicken and remaining cheese. Then gently fold in rest of egg whites.

Turn mixture into mold and set in center of hot oven. Immediately reduce heat to 375°F and bake for 25 to 30 minutes or until soufflé has puffed and browned. Serve immediately.

curried chicken

Yield: 4 servings

1 (3-pound) fryer, cut into serving
    pieces (remove skin on large
    pieces)
2 tablespoons vegetable oil
1 large onion, chopped
½ pound mushrooms, thinly sliced
1 clove garlic, minced
1 tablespoon curry powder

3 tablespoons flour
½ cup white wine
1 cup chicken broth or bouillon
⅛ teaspoon thyme
½ teaspoon salt
⅛ teaspoon pepper
2 firm apples
¼ cup yogurt

In a large frypan, brown chicken pieces in hot oil. Place on platter.

In same frypan, sauté onion and mushrooms. Stir garlic, curry powder, and flour into onion–mushroom mixture. Add wine, broth, thyme, salt, and pepper. Stir and cook until mixture starts to simmer. Add chicken pieces and simmer, covered, for 50 minutes or until done.

Core apples and chop. (Do not peel.) Cook in small covered saucepan until soft. Add apples and yogurt to chicken mixture. Heat through but do not boil.

chicken with mushrooms and celery

Yield: 4 servings

2 tablespoons vegetable oil
1 small onion, sliced
3 stalks celery, cut into ¼-inch
   slices
¼ pound whole mushrooms;
   quarter if large
1 broiler-fryer chicken, skinned,
   boned, and cut into bite-size
   pieces

¾ cup chicken broth or bouillon
2 teaspoons soy sauce
1½ tablespoons cornstarch in 2
   tablespoons water
2 tablespoons dry sherry (optional)

Heat oil in frypan (or wok) and stir-fry onion and celery for 3 minutes. Remove and reserve. Add mushrooms to frypan and stir-fry for 2 minutes. Remove and reserve with onion. Stir-fry chicken 4 to 5 minutes or until done. Return vegetables to pan. Add rest of ingredients and heat until sauce is thickened. Stir constantly. Serve immediately with rice.

pineapple chicken with sweet-and-sour sauce

Yield: 4 servings

1 tablespoon vegetable oil
1 green pepper, cut into thin strips
1 broiler-fryer chicken, skinned,
   boned, and cut into bite-size
   pieces
1 8-ounce can pineapple chunks,
   drained

sauce

¾ cup chicken broth
¼ cup reserved syrup from canned
   pineapple
2 tablespoons dry white wine
1 tablespoon vinegar
1 tablespoon cornstarch in 2
   tablespoons cold water
1 tablespoon orange marmalade
1 tablespoon soy sauce
1 teaspoon grated gingerroot

Heat oil in fry pan (or wok) and stir-fry green pepper for 2 minutes. Remove and reserve. Add chicken to pan and stir-fry 3 to 4 minutes or until done. Return green pepper to pan and add pineapple.

Combine ingredients for sauce and add to the chicken–pineapple mixture. Heat until the sauce boils and is thickened. Serve with rice.

clockwise from top:
shrimp with cauliflower and chicken
pineapple chicken with sweet-and-sour sauce
chicken with mushrooms and celery

curried turkey

Yield: 6 servings

3 turkey legs and thighs, cut at joint into serving pieces
2 tablespoons seasoned flour (add ½ teaspoon salt and ¼ teaspoon pepper)
2 onions, sliced
3 tablespoons vegetable oil

1 apple, peeled, cored, and chopped
1 tablespoon curry powder
2 cups chicken broth
1 tablespoon lemon juice
2 tablespoons chutney
4 tomatoes, chopped

Coat turkey pieces with seasoned flour.

Sauté onions in hot oil until soft in a large frypan or Dutch oven. Add turkey pieces and fry until golden brown. Stir in chopped apple and curry powder. Cook 2 minutes. Add broth, lemon juice, chutney, and tomatoes; mix well. Cover, and simmer for 1 hour or more. Cooking time will vary according to the size of the turkey pieces. Serve with rice.

To reduce calories, remove skin from turkey before cooking.

turkey slices on vegetable bed

Yield: 4 servings

1 tablespoon polyunsaturated margarine
8 ounces fresh small mushrooms
2 10-ounce packages frozen peas, defrosted
4 small tomatoes, peeled and halved
2 tablespoons chopped parsley
½ teaspoon salt
2 tablespoons vegetable oil
4 thick slices cooked turkey breast
Seasonings to taste

Melt margarine in a 2-quart saucepan; add whole mushrooms and sauté lightly. Add peas; cover, and heat gently for 3 minutes. Add tomatoes and parsley; simmer for another 3 minutes. Season with salt.

In a separate pan, heat oil and sauté turkey slices for 2 to 3 minutes on each side or until golden brown. Season to taste.

Arrange vegetables on a heated platter. (Use a slotted spoon if too much liquid has accumulated.) Arrange turkey slices on top of vegetables.

curried turkey

fish steaks seville

Yield: 4 to 6 servings

⅓ cup chopped green pepper
¼ cup chopped onion
1 clove garlic, minced
2 tablespoons vegetable oil
1 16-ounce can tomatoes
2 teaspoons chili powder
½ teaspoon salt

¼ teaspoon pepper
1 bay leaf
1 teaspoon cornstarch
1 tablespoon water
2 pounds fresh or frozen halibut
   steaks

Sauté green pepper, onion, and garlic in hot oil until softened. Add tomatoes, chili powder, salt, pepper, and bay leaf. Simmer for 5 minutes.

Blend cornstarch with water and gradually stir into the hot sauce. Cook, stirring constantly, until thickened and bubbling.

Arrange fish steaks in a greased baking dish. Pour the sauce over the fish. Bake in a preheated 350°F oven for 30 minutes or until the fish is done. Lift the fish from the pan with a pancake turner.

flounder a l'orange

Yield: 6 servings

1 teaspoon salt
Dash pepper
2 tablespoons orange juice
1 teaspoon grated orange rind
2 tablespoons vegetable oil
1½ pounds flounder fillets, cut
   into 6 serving pieces
⅛ teaspoon nutmeg

Combine salt, pepper, orange juice, orange rind, and vegetable oil.

Place fish in an oiled shallow pan and pour sauce on top of fish. Sprinkle with nutmeg and bake in a preheated 350°F oven for 20 to 30 minutes.

picture on opposite page: turkey slices on vegetable bed

savory shrimp soup

savory shrimp soup

Yield: 4 servings

1 medium onion, chopped	1 10-ounce package frozen peas
1 large carrot, chopped	Salt and pepper to taste
1 tablespoon dry white wine	12 ounces medium cooked
1 tablespoon water	shrimps, canned or frozen
3 cups hot beef bouillon	½ cup white wine
1 teaspoon sage	¼ cup skim evaporated milk
1 teaspoon tarragon	

In a 4-quart saucepan or Dutch oven, cook onion and carrot in 1 tablespoon wine and water until onion is soft. Add bouillon and simmer for 12 minutes. Add sage, tarragon, and green peas; bring to a boil and simmer for 8 minutes.

Puree vegetable–bouillon mixture in a blender or food mill and return to pan. Season to taste with salt and pepper. Add shrimps and heat without boiling for about 2 minutes. Stir in ½ cup white wine and the evaporated milk. Correct seasonings and serve immediately.

bouillabaisse (seafood stew)

Yield: 6 servings

sauce

1 tablespoon dry vermouth
2 tablespoons water
2 onions, chopped, or 3 leeks,
    sliced
4 cloves garlic, crushed
2 fresh tomatoes, peeled and diced
3 tablespoons tomato paste
2 cups bottled clam juice
4 cups chicken bouillon
1 tablespoon salt
$\frac{1}{8}$ teaspoon pepper
$\frac{1}{4}$ teaspoon saffron
$\frac{1}{2}$ teaspoon thyme
1 bay leaf
6 sprigs parsley
Grated rind of 1 orange

seafoods

1 (2-pound) lobster or other shellfish, such as clams, scallops, or crab
2 pounds assorted white fish fillets, such as sea bass, perch, cod, sole,
    flounder, or red snapper
Chopped parsley for garnish

In a large saucepan or Dutch oven, add vermouth and 2 tablespoons water and sauté onions or leeks several minutes, until translucent. Add remaining sauce ingredients, and simmer 30 minutes.

Prepare seafoods by cooking lobster. (Place in a large kettle of boiling salted water for 10 minutes.) Break claws and tail from body; crack claws, and cut tail into 1-inch chunks. Remove black vein from tail pieces; leave shell on meat. Wash and cut fish fillets into 2-inch pieces.

Add lobster and firm-fleshed fish (sea bass, perch, etc.) to boiling sauce. Boil rapidly for 5 minutes and then add the tender-fleshed fish, such as clams, scallops, sole, or cod. Boil another 5 minutes. Lift seafoods out as soon as cooked and keep them warm in soup tureen or platter.

Boil liquid for 10 minutes to reduce. Strain liquid through a coarse sieve into tureen, mashing through some of the vegetables. Garnish with parsley and serve.

fish fillets on spinach

fish fillets on spinach

Yield: 6 servings

1½ pounds fish fillets
Juice of 1 lemon
2 pounds fresh spinach
2 tablespoons vegetable oil
1 medium onion, chopped
1 teaspoon polyunsaturated
   margarine

½ teaspoon salt
⅛ teaspoon white pepper
½ teaspoon grated fresh nutmeg
2 tomatoes, peeled
¼ cup grated low-fat mozzarella
   cheese

Wash fish and pat dry. Sprinkle with lemon juice and let stand for 10 minutes.

Wash spinach well and chop coarsely.

Heat oil in frypan, add onion, and sauté until soft. Fry fish in pan with onions for a few minutes on each side until golden brown. Remove fish and onions and reserve.

Add spinach to frypan and stir-fry for 4 to 5 minutes.

Grease a casserole dish with margarine. Add spinach. Arrange fish fillets on top of spinach and sprinkle with salt, pepper, and nutmeg. Place peeled and sliced tomatoes on top of fish. Sprinkle with grated cheese. Bake in preheated 350°F oven for 15 minutes.

88

fish with lemon sauce

fish with lemon sauce

Yield: 4 servings

1½ pounds fish fillets
Juice of 1 lemon
2 medium onions, chopped
2 tablespoons vegetable oil
½ teaspoon salt
⅛ teaspoon white pepper
½ cup water
2 thin slices fresh gingerroot

¼ teaspoon mace
Grated rind of 1 lemon
¼ cup lemon juice
1 tablespoon cornstarch
¼ cup water
¼ teaspoon saffron
¼ cup plain yogurt
Chopped parsley for garnish

Wash fish and pat dry. Sprinkle with juice of 1 lemon and let stand for 10 minutes.

Sauté onions in hot oil until golden brown. Add fish and brown on both sides for about 5 minutes. Add salt, pepper, water, gingerroot, mace, lemon rind, and lemon juice. Simmer, covered, for 10 minutes. Remove fish and keep them warm.

Mix cornstarch with water and stir in fish sauce. Add saffron and simmer sauce for 2 minutes to thicken. Stir in yogurt; remove from heat; garnish and serve immediately.

marinated fish fillets

Yield: 6 servings

1½ pounds fish fillets

marinade

**2 tablespoons vegetable oil
¼ cup tarragon vinegar
1 teaspoon salt
1 teaspoon Worcestershire sauce
¼ teaspoon pepper
1 bay leaf
2 teaspoons tarragon**

Combine marinade ingredients in a shallow dish. Add fish; cover, and refrigerate for 4 hours or more. Turn fish occasionally to keep both sides moist.

Remove from the marinade. Place on a broiler pan and broil 3 inches from the flame for 15 minutes or until the fish is done.

fish neopolitan

Yield: 4 servings

**2 tablespoons water
1 onion, chopped
3 tablespoons chopped green
pepper
1 tablespoon chopped parsley
2 medium tomatoes, cut in pieces
½ cup tomato juice
1 tablespoon chopped black olives
½ teaspoon salt
½ teaspoon basil
⅛ teaspoon pepper
1 pound fish fillets**

Heat 2 tablespoons water in a large frypan and cook onion for 2 to 3 minutes, until tender. Add the rest of the ingredients except the fish and cook until the tomatoes and green pepper are soft, about 10 minutes. Add the fish. Cover, and simmer gently about 10 minutes or until fish is flaky.

baked cod

Yield: 4 servings

**1 dressed fresh cod, about 2
    pounds**
3 lemons
4 tomatoes, sliced
1 pound whole mushrooms
½ teaspoon salt
⅛ teaspoon pepper
½ teaspoon marjoram
½ teaspoon thyme
1 bay leaf
1 large onion
3 tablespoons vegetable oil

Wash fish, pat dry, and place in a baking dish. Sprinkle the juice of 1 lemon over the fish. Garnish with the tomatoes and the remaining lemons cut into slices.

Wash the mushrooms and place around the fish. Season with salt and pepper. Add marjoram, thyme, and bay leaf.

Cut the onion into rings and add. Sprinkle with cooking oil. Bake covered (foil or lid) 15 minutes in preheated 325°F oven. Remove cover and continue cooking for 10 to 15 minutes or until fish flakes.

picture on next pages: baked cod

trout in lemon aspic

Yield: 4 servings

4 whole fresh lake trout (scaled,
    viscerated, and cleaned)
1½ cups white wine
1 cup chicken consommé
3 tablespoons lemon juice
2 tablespoons dry sherry
1 small onion, cut into rings

3 sprigs parsley
1½ envelopes unflavored gelatin
    (1½ tablespoons)
¼ cup water
¼ cup chopped parsley
1 lemon, thinly sliced and seeds
    removed

Place the trout in a 12-inch baking dish. Add the white wine, consommé, lemon juice, sherry, onion, and parsley sprigs. Cover with lid or foil and gently simmer until fish flakes (about 20 minutes).

While fish is cooking, soak gelatin in cold water.

Lift the trout from the baking dish and carefully remove the skin. Discard parsley sprigs from stock and add gelatin mixture and chopped parsley. Heat again until hot but not boiling.

Pour the aspic into a serving dish and allow to cool slightly. Arrange the fish in the serving dish before the aspic has set. Place 2 onion rings on top of each trout. Arrange the lemon slices in the dish, and spoon the aspic over all. Chill for 4 hours before serving. Serve with Lemon Sauce (see Index).

broiled scallops

Yield: 6 servings

1½ pounds fresh or frozen
    scallops, defrosted
2 tablespoons honey
2 tablespoons prepared mustard
1 teaspoon curry powder
1 teaspoon lemon juice
Lemon slices

Rinse scallops and pat dry with paper towels.

Combine honey, mustard, curry, and lemon juice.

Place scallops on a broiler pan and brush with coating. Broil at 425°F, 4 inches from the flame, for 8 to 10 minutes or until lightly browned. Turn scallops and brush with remaining sauce. Broil 8 to 10 minutes longer. Garnish with lemon slices.

fish steaks with shrimp sauce

Yield: 4 servings

4 fish steaks (each 6 to 8 ounces)
Juice of 1 lemon
½ teaspoon salt
¼ teaspoon white pepper
2 tablespoons polyunsaturated
    margarine
1 medium onion, sliced
1 tablespoon chopped parsley
½ cup dry white wine

½ cup beef bouillon
6 ounces fresh mushrooms, sliced
¼ pound frozen cooked shrimps
1 tablespoon lemon juice
¼ cup plain yogurt
Lemon slices and parsley for
    garnish

Wash fish, pat dry, and sprinkle with lemon juice, salt, and pepper.

Heat margarine in a frypan, add fish and onion and brown fish for 5 minutes on each side. Sprinkle with parsley, pour in white wine, and simmer for 5 minutes. Remove fish to a heated platter and keep them warm.

Add bouillon to frypan and bring to boil. Add mushrooms and simmer slowly for 8 minutes, stirring often. Add shrimps and simmer for 2 to 3 minutes. Season sauce with lemon juice, and stir in yogurt. Heat thoroughly, but do not boil. Adjust seasonings.

Pour over fish steaks and garnish with lemon slices and parsley.

fish steaks with shrimp sauce

mediterranean fish stew

Yield: 4 servings

broth

> **1 large fish head**
> **1 bay leaf**
> **1 medium onion, chopped**
> **½ teaspoon salt**
> **¼ teaspoon white pepper**
> **6 cups water**

stew

> **1 large onion, chopped**
> **1 clove garlic, minced**
> **1 tablespoon white wine**
> **1 tablespoon water**
> **3 medium potatoes, peeled and**
> **cubed**
> **1 pound white fish fillets, cut into**
> **cubes**
> **2 tablespoons lemon juice**
> **3 medium tomatoes, peeled and**
> **chopped**
> **¼ cup stuffed green olives**
> **1 tablespoon capers**
> **Salt and white pepper to taste**
> **Chopped parsley for garnish**

In a 4-quart saucepan, combine ingredients for broth and simmer for 1 hour. Strain and reserve broth.

Meanwhile, cook onion and garlic in wine and water until soft. Add fish broth and potatoes; simmer for 30 minutes.

While potatoes are cooking, sprinkle fish with lemon juice and add to broth 10 minutes before end of cooking time. After 5 minutes add tomatoes, olives, and capers. Season stew to taste and sprinkle with chopped parsley.

picture on opposite page: mediterranean fish stew

shrimp risotto

Yield: 4 servings

    1 pound shrimps
    3 cups water
    1 small onion, chopped
    1 tablespoon water
    1 tablespoon dry vermouth
    1½ cups uncooked rice
    1 stalk celery, chopped
    ¼ pound fresh mushrooms, sliced
    1 red or green pepper, sliced
    1 package frozen peas, thawed
    ¼ teaspoon saffron

stock

    2 small onions, sliced
    ½ stalk celery, chopped
    1 clove garlic, minced
    1 cup white wine
    ½ teaspoon salt
    ¼ teaspoon pepper

garnish

    1 tablespoon finely chopped parsley
    ¼ cup grated Parmesan cheese

Peel and devein shrimps. Put stock ingredients plus shrimp peels and 3 cups water in a 1½-quart saucepan. Simmer for 20 minutes and strain.

In a large saucepan, cook onion in 1 tablespoon water and vermouth until translucent. Add rice and strained stock. Cover, and simmer for 15 minutes. Add celery, mushrooms, green pepper, peas, and saffron. Cover, and simmer gently for 10 minutes. Add shrimps, bring to a boil, boil for 3 to 5 minutes, and serve.

Transfer food to a hot serving dish; garnish with parsley and cheese.

shrimp risotto

shrimp with cauliflower and chicken

Yield: 4 servings

1 tablespoon vegetable oil
1½ cups cauliflower, cut into
    florets and parboiled (cover
    with boiling water and let
    stand 5 minutes)
½ cup peas, fresh, or frozen and
    defrosted
½ pound cooked chicken, cubed
1 pound whole shrimps, cooked
2 scallions, cut lengthwise into
    thin strips

sauce
¾ cup chicken broth
1 tablespoon soy sauce
2 tablespoons chili sauce
1 tablespoon cornstarch in 2
    tablespoons cold water
2 tablespoons dry white wine

Heat oil in frypan (or wok if available) and stir-fry cauliflower florets 2 minutes. Remove and reserve.

Stir-fry peas for 2 minutes; reserve with cauliflower.

Add chicken, shrimps, and scallions to frypan. Stir-fry 2 to 3 minutes, until heated. Return vegetables to pan.

Combine sauce ingredients and add to pan. Heat until the sauce boils and thickens. Serve with rice.

neopolitan fish chowder

Yield: 4 to 6 servings

1 medium onion, chopped
2 carrots, thinly sliced
2 tablespoons minced parsley
1 clove garlic, minced
2 tablespoons vegetable oil
¼ teaspoon pepper
½ teaspoon salt

1 can (8 ounces) tomato sauce
2 cups hot water
1 small can whole baby clams (or
    minced clams)
1 pound fish fillets, cut in 1-inch
    pieces

In a large frypan, sauté onion, carrots, parsley, and garlic in hot oil until onion is soft. Add pepper, salt, tomato sauce, and 2 cups hot water. Bring to boil. Add clams with liquid and fish. Cover, and simmer about 30 minutes.

shrimp in garlic sauce

shrimp in garlic sauce

Yield: 4 servings

1 tablespoon vegetable oil
1 small onion, chopped
1 teaspoon freshly grated
    gingerroot
3 cloves garlic, minced
4 Chinese dried black mushrooms
    (soaked 30 minutes in warm
    water, drained, and sliced)

½ cup peas, fresh, or frozen and
    defrosted
1 pound cooked shrimps
1 cup chicken broth
2 teaspoons soy sauce
1 tablespoon cornstarch blended
    with 2 tablespoons water

Heat oil in frypan (or wok if available) and stir-fry onion, ginger, and garlic. Mix in mushrooms and peas and stir-fry 2 to 3 minutes. Add shrimps and continue stir-frying 1 to 2 minutes.

Combine broth, soy sauce, and cornstarch. Add to shrimp mixture and heat until the sauce boils and thickens. Serve at once over boiled rice.

vegetables

turkish eggplant

Yield: 4 servings

4 small eggplants
3 tablespoons vegetable oil
2 medium onions, sliced
3 tomatoes, peeled and sliced
2 cloves garlic, minced
½ teaspoon salt
1 tablespoon chopped parsley
1 bay leaf
1 cinnamon stick
⅛ teaspoon white pepper
8 black olives
8 rolled anchovy fillets

turkish eggplant

Remove stems and approximately ½-inch slice from tops of eggplants (see picture).

Heat 2 tablespoons of the oil in a frypan and fry eggplants on all sides for 5 minutes. Remove eggplants from pan, cool slightly, and scoop out pulp, leaving a shell approximately 1 inch thick.

Heat 1 tablespoon oil in same pan, add onions, and sauté lightly. Stir in tomatoes and simmer for 5 minutes. Add garlic, salt, parsley, bay leaf, cinnamon stick, and white pepper. Cook for another 5 minutes; remove bay leaf and cinnamon.

Arrange eggplant shells in a greased baking dish and fill with vegetable mixture. Bake in a preheated oven, 350°F, for 15 minutes. Garnish with olives and anchovies.

glazed turnips

Yield: 6 servings

2 pounds turnips, peeled and
    quartered
2 tablespoons vegetable oil
1 to 1½ cups beef bouillon

1 tablespoon polyunsaturated
    margarine
3 tablespoons sugar
2 tablespoons minced parsley

Blanch the turnips in boiling salted water to cover for 5 minutes. Drain and pat dry with paper towels. Sauté the turnips in hot oil for 3 minutes to lightly brown. Pour in bouillon to barely cover. Add margarine and sugar. Cover, and boil slowly for 20 to 30 minutes or until turnips are just tender. Uncover, and boil the liquid down to reduce to a thick syrup. Gently top the turnips and coat with the glaze.

Place in a vegetable dish or around a roast and sprinkle with parsley.

eggplant parmesan

Yield: 6 servings

1 medium eggplant
½ teaspoon salt
2 egg whites, slightly beaten
¼ cup bread crumbs
3 tablespoons vegetable oil
2 tomatoes, sliced thin
½ pound fresh mushrooms, sliced
1 cup tomato sauce
½ pound sliced mozzarella cheese
    (low fat)

Peel eggplant and cut into ½-inch slices. Sprinkle with salt and let stand for 1 hour. Rinse with cold water. Pound eggplant slices to ¼ inch thickness. (Use a meat mallet or edge of a saucer.) Dip eggplant slices in egg whites and then in bread crumbs. Sauté in hot vegetable oil and drain on paper towels.

Arrange eggplant in the bottom of an ovenproof baking dish. Place a layer of tomato slices on the eggplant, followed by a layer of mushrooms. Pour tomato sauce over all, and arrange cheese on top. Bake at 450°F for 20 minutes. If desired, brown cheese under the broiler for a minute or two at the end of the cooking time.

white asparagus in white sauce

white asparagus in white sauce

Yield: 4 servings

> 2 14½-ounce cans white asparagus
> 2 tablespoons polyunsaturated
>   margarine
> 2 tablespoons flour
> ½ cup reserved liquid (from
>   asparagus)
> ½ cup skim milk
> 4 ounces cooked lean ham, cut into
>   julienne strips
> ⅛ teaspoon nutmeg (freshly
>   ground if possible)
> ¼ teaspoon salt

Drain asparagus spears, reserving ½ cup of liquid.

Heat margarine in a saucepan. Add flour and blend. Gradually pour in asparagus liquid and milk. Stir constantly over low heat until sauce thickens and bubbles. Add ham and seasonings. Gently stir in asparagus spears and heat through, but do not boil. Serve in a preheated serving dish.

tangy broccoli

Yield: 3 to 4 servings

**1 pound fresh broccoli (or 1
   10-ounce package frozen
   broccoli, thawed)**
1 tablespoon vegetable oil
¼ teaspoon dry mustard
½ teaspoon salt
⅛ teaspoon pepper
3 tablespoons water
½ teaspoon dillseed

Trim and wash fresh broccoli. Do not dry.

In a saucepan with a tight-fitting cover, add oil, broccoli, dry mustard, salt, pepper, water, and dillseed. Cover, and cook over medium heat for about 15 minutes or until tender. If frozen broccoli is used, separate stalks with a fork during first few minutes of cooking. Shake pan occasionally to prevent sticking and cook until just tender.

artichokes provençale

Yield: 4 servings

1 tablespoon vegetable oil
**½ cup canned artichoke bottoms,
   quartered (with liquid)**
1 cup frozen peas
¼ teaspoon garlic salt
¼ teaspoon salt
⅛ teaspoon pepper
½ cup shredded endive

Heat the oil and add all the ingredients. Cook covered over low heat until the peas are done. Stir occasionally and add a tablespoon or two of water if needed.

glazed carrots with herbs

Yield: 4 servings

8 carrots
1 teaspoon salt
2 teaspoons sugar
2 tablespoons polyunsaturated
  margarine
1½ cups water, or enough to cover
2 teaspoons minced parsley
1 teaspoon chopped chives

Peel carrots and place in a saucepan with salt, sugar, margarine, and water to cover. Bring carrots to a boil and simmer until done. Leave pan uncovered and liquids will evaporate to a thick syrup. Top the carrots occasionally to coat with the sauce.

When carrots are tender and a small amount of syrup remains, place carrots in a serving dish and sprinkle with parsley and chives.

acorn squash with applesauce filling

Yield: 4 servings

2 acorn squashes, cut in half
1 cup unsweetened applesauce
2 teaspoons brown sugar
2 tablespoons raisins
2 teaspoons polyunsaturated
  margarine

Preheat oven to 400°F.

Remove seeds from squashes and place halves cut side down in a shallow baking pan. Add water to cover ½ inch of squash. Bake for 50 to 60 minutes or until tender. Turn squash over. Fill each cavity with a mixture of applesauce, brown sugar, and raisins. Dot with margarine. Continue baking 15 to 20 minutes or until the applesauce bubbles.

italian-style yellow squash

Yield: 6 servings

   **1 tablespoon polyunsaturated
       margarine**
   **3 small onions, peeled and cut into
       thin strips**
   **1 pound (3 small) yellow squash,
       sliced crosswise**
   **3 medium tomatoes, each cut into 8
       wedges**
   **1 green pepper, seeded and cut
       into thin strips**
   ½ teaspoon salt
   ¼ teaspoon white pepper
   1 teaspoon sugar
   ¼ teaspoon allspice

Melt margarine and cook onions until tender. Add remaining vegetables and seasonings. Mix well. Cover, and simmer for 10 minutes, until squash is tender.

zucchini and cheese bake

Yield: 4 servings

   **2 medium zucchini squashes,
       sliced**
   1 small onion, chopped
   2 tablespoons vegetable oil
   ½ pound low-fat cottage cheese
   ½ teaspoon basil
   2 tablespoons Parmesan cheese

Sauté zucchini and onion in hot oil. Drain.
Puree cottage cheese and basil in a blender.
Alternate layers of cheese and zucchini in a greased ovenproof casserole dish. Sprinkle Parmesan cheese on top. Bake uncovered at 350°F for 20 to 25 minutes.

green peas bonne femme

Yield: 6 servings

    **¼ pound Canadian bacon, cut in
       1-inch pieces**
**1 tablespoon polyunsaturated
      margarine**
3 cups fresh green peas
6 small white onions, peeled
Inner leaves of lettuce head
½ cup water
½ teaspoon salt
¼ teaspoon pepper
½ teaspoon sugar
**1 tablespoon finely chopped
      parsley**

Fry bacon in margarine until lightly browned. Add peas, onions, lettuce, water, salt, pepper, and sugar. Cover, and cook for 10 to 15 minutes or until peas are tender. When peas are done, drain remaining liquid. Sprinkle with parsley before serving.

sherried peas and mushrooms

Yield: 4 servings

    1 4-ounce can sliced mushrooms
**1 tablespoon polyunsaturated
      margarine**
⅛ teaspoon marjoram
⅛ teaspoon nutmeg
2 tablespoons sherry
1 10-ounce package frozen peas

Drain mushrooms, reserving liquid.

In a frypan, melt margarine and sauté mushrooms slightly. Stir in marjoram, nutmeg, and sherry. Break apart frozen peas and pour into the pan with the mushrooms. Turn off the heat; cover, and let stand for several minutes. Just before serving, add 2 tablespoons of reserved mushroom liquid and bring to a boil, stirring occasionally.

green peas bonne femme

seasoned green beans

Yield: 4 servings

**1 tablespoon polyunsaturated
    margarine**
2 tablespoons water
½ teaspoon salt
**1 9-ounce package frozen
    French-style green beans**
½ cup finely chopped celery
¼ cup finely chopped onion
1 tablespoon chopped pimiento
1 tablespoon vinegar
¼ teaspoon dillseed
⅛ teaspoon pepper

Measure margarine, water, and salt in a saucepan. Bring to a boil and add frozen beans. Cook over low heat, stirring often to separate beans. Cover, and cook until tender. Additional water may be necessary. Add remaining ingredients, toss lightly, and heat for 2 to 3 minutes. Celery and onion will be crisp.

green beans with radishes

Yield: 4 servings

**2 tablespoons polyunsaturated
    margarine**
1 tablespoon chopped scallions
1 teaspoon lemon juice
1 teaspoon soy sauce
¼ cup sliced radishes
**1 16-ounce can cut green beans,
    drained**
2 tablespoons slivered almonds

Melt margarine in a frypan. Sauté scallions until softened. Stir in lemon juice, soy sauce, and radishes; cook, stirring often, for 5 minutes. Add beans, and heat through. Gently stir in almonds and serve.

green beans with parmesan cheese

Yield: 4 servings

1 pound fresh green beans
½ cup water
1 teaspoon salt
¼ cup freshly grated Parmesan
    cheese
2 tablespoons polyunsaturated
    margarine
2 tablespoons finely chopped
    parsley
Freshly ground black pepper

Wash and trim beans. Place in a saucepan with water and salt; bring to a simmer. Cook for 3 minutes with the cover off to retain bright-green color of beans. Then cover, and simmer until just tender—about 20 minutes. Drain, sprinkle with cheese, and dot with margarine. Cook uncovered for 2 minutes. Sprinkle with parsley and season with pepper.

lemon potatoes

Yield: 6 servings

4 baking potatoes
1 large onion, chopped
1 tablespoon flour
2 tablespoons margarine
¼ cup fresh, chopped parsley
¼ teaspoon nutmeg
½ teaspoon salt
⅛ teaspoon pepper
Grated rind and juice of 1 lemon

Peel potatoes and cut into large pieces. Boil in salted water for 5 minutes. Drain. Toss with remaining ingredients except lemon juice.

Place potatoes in an ovenproof casserole; cover, and bake at 450°F until the potatoes are tender, about 50 minutes. Sprinkle lemon juice over the top just before serving.

green beans provençale

Yield: 4 to 6 servings

1 cup thinly sliced onions
2 tablespoons vegetable oil
4 large tomatoes, peeled, seeded,
   and chopped
2 cloves garlic, crushed
3 parsley sprigs
1 bay leaf
½ teaspoon thyme
½ cup water
½ teaspoon salt
⅛ teaspoon pepper
2 pounds fresh cut green beans or 2
   10-ounce packages cut green
   beans, defrosted
½ teaspoon tarragon
1 tablespoon parsley

Cook the onions slowly in hot vegetable oil until tender and translucent but not browned, about 10 minutes. Add tomatoes, garlic, parsley sprigs, bay leaf, thyme, water, salt, and pepper. Simmer, covered, for 30 minutes. Remove parsley sprigs and bay leaf.

Meanwhile, if fresh green beans are used, blanch in large pan with 6 quarts of boiling salted water for about 10 minutes. Drain beans just before done. Add beans, fresh or frozen, to pan with onions and tomatoes. Cover, and simmer slowly for 8 to 10 minutes, stirring occasionally until tender. If most of the liquid has not evaporated, uncover, and raise heat slightly. Correct seasoning, stir in tarragon and parsley, and serve.

beets with apples

Yield: 4 servings

1½ cups chopped cooked beets
1½ cups chopped tart apples
¼ cup thinly sliced onions
½ teaspoon salt

¼ teaspoon nutmeg
1 tablespoon polyunsaturated
   margarine

Mix beets, apples, onions, salt, and nutmeg. Place in a greased ovenproof casserole. Dot with margarine; cover, and bake in a preheated 325°F oven for 1 hour.

fennel italian

Yield: 4 servings

1 pound small fennel roots
1 tablespoon water
1 cup dry white wine
2 medium tomatoes, peeled and
   quartered
Salt, white pepper, and paprika to
   taste
Parsley for garnish

Clean fennel thoroughly and cut in quarters. Cook fennel in 1 tablespoon water and 2 tablespoons wine for 5 minutes, stirring often. (Add more wine if necessary.) Add tomatoes, rest of wine, and seasonings. Cover and simmer for 30 minutes or until fennel is tender. Gently stir vegetables occasionally. Correct seasonings, and serve on a heated platter. Garnish with parsley.

fennel italian

braised celery

Yield: 4 servings

1 bunch celery
½ teaspoon salt
¼ teaspoon pepper
2 tablespoons polyunsaturated
    margarine

1 chicken bouillon cube, dissolved
    in 1 cup boiling water
1 tablespoon finely chopped
    parsley

Remove green leaves from celery and cut stalks in 4-inch lengths. Arrange stalks in bottom of a small pan or heat-proof casserole. Season with salt and pepper. Dot with margarine, and pour chicken bouillon over celery. Bring the liquid to a boil, cover pan or casserole, and simmer for 30 minutes or until celery is tender.

Place on heated serving dish and sprinkle with parsley.

boiled beets in yogurt

Yield: 4 servings

3 cups cooked or canned sliced
    beets
½ cup plain yogurt
1 tablespoon prepared horseradish
1 tablespoon chopped chives
1 teaspoon grated onion

Combine all ingredients in the top of a double boiler. Heat thoroughly. Season to taste, and serve.

beets horseradish

Yield: 4 to 6 servings

½ cup plain yogurt
¼ cup prepared horseradish
1 teaspoon sugar
¼ teaspoon salt

Dash cayenne pepper
1 16-ounce can diced beets, drained
1 or 2 scallions, chopped

Combine yogurt, horseradish, sugar, salt, and cayenne pepper. Fold beets into yogurt mixture. Chill. Garnish with scallions to serve.

cheese-stuffed tomatoes

cheese-stuffed tomatoes

Yield: 4 servings

4 medium tomatoes
2 ounces blue cheese
2 ounces low-fat cottage cheese
2 tablespoons evaporated skim
  milk
1 stalk celery
¼ teaspoon salt
¼ teaspoon paprika
½ teaspoon chopped chives
4 lettuce leaves

Wash tomatoes and slice off tops. Scoop out seeds.
Crumble blue cheese with a fork and blend with cottage cheese and milk.
Mince celery and add to cheese. Season with salt and paprika.
Fill tomatoes with cheese mixture. Sprinkle chopped chives over the top.
Place tomato tops back on and serve on lettuce leaves.

115

ratatouille

Yield: 4 servings

1½ pounds zucchini
1 medium eggplant
1 red pepper
1 green pepper
3 tomatoes
1 large onion
1 clove garlic
2 tablespoons vegetable oil
½ teaspoon salt
¼ teaspoon white pepper
½ teaspoon rosemary
½ teaspoon basil

Cut zucchini in 1-inch slices; cube eggplant and peppers. Peel tomatoes and chop coarsely. Chop onion and garlic.

Heat oil in a Dutch oven; add onion and garlic, and sauté until tender. Add vegetables and season with salt, pepper, rosemary, and basil. Cover pan and bake vegetables in a preheated 350°F oven for 45 minutes.

oriental vegetables

Yield: 4 servings

1 tablespoon vegetable oil
¼ cup blanched almonds, slivered
2 green peppers, sliced into ¼-inch
    strips
2 scallions, cut into thin strips
    about 2 inches in length
1 onion, thinly sliced
1 8-ounce can bamboo shoots,
    sliced
Soy sauce to taste

Heat oil in frypan (or wok if available). Stir-fry almonds 1 to 2 minutes or until lightly browned. Remove from pan and reserve. One at a time, stir-fry vegetables for 1 to 2 minutes each. Remove each vegetable when done. After all vegetables have been cooked, return vegetables to pan. Add soy sauce to taste. Return almonds to pan and serve.

ratatouille

baked stuffed tomatoes

Yield: 4 servings

4 firm, red tomatoes
½ teaspoon salt
⅛ teaspoon pepper
1 clove garlic, mashed
3 tablespoons minced green onions

1 teaspoon dried basil
2 teaspoons dried parsley
⅛ teaspoon thyme
½ cup fine, dry bread crumbs
2 tablespoons oil

Preheat oven to 400°F.

Core tomatoes and cut slice off tops. With a knife, gently press out the juice and seeds. Sprinkle with salt and pepper.

Mix together the rest of the ingredients. Fill each tomato with a spoonful or two of the mixture.

Arrange in a small greased pan and bake for about 15 minutes. Tomatoes should be tender but holding their shape.

tomatoes rockefeller

Yield: 6 servings

3 large tomatoes, cut in half and
    seeds removed
2 tablespoons finely chopped
    onion
1 tablespoon finely chopped
    parsley
2 tablespoons polyunsaturated
    margarine
½ cup chopped cooked spinach,
    drained well
¼ teaspoon salt
⅛ teaspoon pepper
¼ teaspoon paprika
2 tablespoons bread crumbs

Place tomatoes in a shallow baking dish, cut side up.

Mix the rest of the ingredients except bread crumbs. Divide and spread evenly over tomatoes. Top with crumbs. Bake in a preheated 375°F oven for 15 minutes or until the crumbs are toasted and tomato is heated.

health salad

Yield: 4 to 6 servings

1 head Boston lettuce
1 small cucumber
2 small tomatoes
1 green pepper
½ avocado
5 radishes
1 peach
1 slice pineapple (from can)
4 ounces mandarin oranges (from can)
¼ pound fresh strawberries

dressing

1 small onion, minced
2 teaspoons prepared mustard
6 tablespoons lemon juice
¼ teaspoon salt
⅛ teaspoon white pepper
3 tablespoons vegetable oil
1 sprig parsley, chopped
2 teaspoons fresh dill (or ½ teaspoon dried dill)
¼ teaspoon dried tarragon
¼ teaspoon dried basil

Wash lettuce and tear leaves in bite-size pieces. Cut unpeeled cucumber in thin slices. Peel tomatoes and cut in slices. Core, seed, and slice green pepper. Peel avocado and slice. Clean radishes and slice. Peel peach and cube peach and pineapple slice. Drain oranges. Hull and cut strawberries in half. Arrange all ingredients in a large bowl.

To make the dressing, blend onion thoroughly with mustard, lemon juice, salt, pepper, and vegetable oil. Add herbs and correct the seasoning if necessary. Pour over the salad; mix gently but thoroughly. Cover salad, and marinate for about 10 minutes. Serve in a bowl or on a platter.

health salad

cabbage fruit salad with yogurt dressing

Yield: 6 servings

2 cups shredded raw cabbage
1 diced apple (red unpeeled)
1 tablespoon lemon juice
½ cup raisins
¼ cup pineapple juice
1½ teaspoons lemon juice
¼ teaspoon salt
1 tablespoon sugar
½ cup yogurt

Shred cabbage. Dice apple and add lemon juice to prevent apple from darkening. Toss together cabbage, apple, and raisins.

Mix together fruit juices, salt, and sugar. Add yogurt, and stir until smooth. Add to salad and chill.

citrus salad

Yield: 6 servings

2 grapefruit
¼ cup vegetable oil
¼ cup tarragon vinegar
1 tablespoon orange marmalade
1 head Bibb lettuce
1 cup chopped watercress

Cut skin and white surface from grapefruit. Section with a knife over a bowl so as to save the juice.

Mix oil, vinegar, marmalade, and grapefruit juices. Pour over grapefruit sections and chill several hours.

Wash and chill greens to crisp. Toss fruit and dressing with greens.

fruit salad with nuts

fruit salad with nuts

Yield: 4 to 6 servings

1 small honeydew melon
2 oranges
1 cup blue grapes
Lettuce leaves
12 walnut halves

dressing

1 8-ounce container yogurt
1 tablespoon lemon juice
1 tablespoon orange juice
1 tablespoon tomato catsup
2 tablespoons evaporated skim
    milk
Dash of salt
Dash of white pepper

Scoop out melon with melon baller. Cut peel from oranges, remove white membrane, and slice crosswise. Cut grapes in half and remove seeds. Line a glass bowl with lettuce leaves; arrange melon balls, orange slices, grapes, and walnuts in layers on top of lettuce.

Mix and blend well all the ingredients for the dressing. Adjust seasonings. Pour dressing over the fruit. Let salad ingredients marinate for 30 minutes. Toss salad just before serving.

pineapple–cucumber salad

Yield: 6 servings

  **1 small cucumber, peeled and
    chopped (about 2 cups)**
  ½ teaspoon salt
  **2 envelopes (2 tablespoons)
    unflavored gelatin**
  ½ cup cold water
  **1½ cups pineapple juice
    (unsweetened)**
  ¼ cup cider vinegar
  1 tablespoon sugar
  **⅛ teaspoon dillweed, slightly
    crushed**
  ½ cup plain yogurt
  **1 can (8 ounces) crushed pineapple,
    drained**

Sprinkle cucumber with the salt and let stand at least 15 minutes. Drain well.

Meanwhile, soften gelatin in ½ cup cold water and then dissolve over simmering water. Add pineapple juice, vinegar, sugar, dillweed, and yogurt. Stir to blend, then chill until slightly thickened. Fold in cucumber and crushed pineapple; pour into a 5-cup mold and chill until firm. Unmold and serve on greens.

cold asparagus with yogurt dressing

Yield: 4 servings

  **2 pounds fresh asparagus, washed
    and trimmed**
  ⅔ cup plain yogurt
  2 tablespoons catsup
  ½ teaspoon salt
  ⅛ teaspoon white pepper
  Dash Worcestershire sauce

Cook asparagus, uncovered, in salted water until tender. Drain; cover, and chill in the refrigerator.

Combine yogurt with catsup, salt, pepper, and Worcestershire sauce. Blend well and chill. Serve over the asparagus.

caribbean salad

Yield: 4 servings

2 tablespoons vinegar
½ teaspoon salt
⅛ teaspoon white pepper
1 teaspoon honey
3 drops angostura bitters
½ small onion, grated
2 tablespoons vegetable oil
2 medium bananas
2 medium tomatoes
**2 mandarin oranges (or 1 small
    can, drained)**
1 4½-ounce can shrimps
Parsley for garnish
4 stuffed olives for garnish

caribbean salad

Make salad dressing by combining and blending vinegar, salt, pepper, honey, bitters, onion, and oil. Adjust seasonings to taste.

Peel and slice bananas and add immediately to dressing to prevent browning. Peel tomatoes and cut into quarters; peel oranges and section (remove all white membrane). Add tomatoes and oranges to dressing. Carefully stir in drained shrimps.

Arrange salad in an attractive bowl and garnish with parsley and stuffed halved olives.

far-east cucumber salad

Yield: 4 servings

2 medium cucumbers
1 tablespoon soy sauce
2 tablespoons vinegar
1 tablespoon oil

Thinly slice unpeeled cucumbers. Add other ingredients and chill for 1 to 2 hours.

spinach salad

Yield: 4 servings

dressing

> **2 tablespoons vegetable oil**
> **Juice of 1 lemon**
> **1 tablespoon Dijon-style mustard**
> **1 tablespoon grated Parmesan**
> **cheese**
> **1 teaspoon sugar**
> **1 teaspoon Worcestershire sauce**
> **½ teaspoon salt**
> **Dash of pepper**

salad

> **1 bunch or 1 package (10-ounce)**
> **fresh spinach**
> **¼ pound fresh mushrooms, sliced**
> **1 hard-cooked egg white, sieved or**
> **chopped**
> **¼ cup sunflower seeds**

Combine dressing ingredients in small jar with lid; shake well and chill.

Thoroughly wash spinach and tear into bite-size pieces. Chill in a tight plastic bag to crisp.

In a large bowl, combine spinach and mushrooms. Toss spinach mixture with dressing. Garnish with egg whites and sunflower seeds.

spinach mushroom italian salad

Yield: 6 to 8 servings

> **2 fresh grapefruit**
> **1 ripe avocado, sliced**
> **1 tablespoon lemon juice**
> **1 10-ounce package fresh spinach,**
> **washed, torn into bite-size**
> **pieces, and chilled**

> **¼ pound fresh mushrooms, thinly**
> **sliced**
> **1 or 2 scallions, finely chopped**
> **½ medium cucumber, thinly sliced**
> **1 stalk celery, thinly sliced**

Peel and section grapefruit; drain sections well to remove excess juice. Dip avocado slices in lemon juice to prevent darkening. At serving time toss ingredients together lightly with a low-calorie Italian dressing.

pineapple salad

pineapple salad

Yield: 4 to 6 servings

2 slices canned pineapple
2 oranges
2 apples
¼ medium melon (honeydew or
cantaloupe)
½ pound green seedless grapes

dressing

½ cup plain yogurt
1 tablespoon imitation mayonnaise
(or low-calorie mayonnaise)
2 tablespoons lemon juice
¼ teaspoon salt
⅛ teaspoon white pepper
1 teaspoon honey

Cut pineapple slices into ½-inch pieces. Peel and section oranges, removing all membranes. Cut sections into pieces. Peel apples and melon, remove seeds, and cut into bite-size pieces. Cut grapes in half. Gently mix fruit in large bowl.

To make the dressing, blend the yogurt, mayonnaise, and lemon juice. Season to taste with salt, pepper, and honey. Pour dressing over the fruit and mix gently. Cover bowl and refrigerate salad for 10 minutes to blend the flavors.

caraway cabbage salad

Yield: 6 to 8 servings

dressing

    1 tablespoon cider vinegar
    1 teaspoon caraway seed
    1 teaspoon prepared mustard
    ½ teaspoon salt
    ⅛ teaspoon garlic salt
    1 cup plain yogurt

salad

    2 medium red apples, unpeeled
        and chopped coarsely
    1 teaspoon lemon juice
    2 cups shredded green cabbage
    2 cups shredded red cabbage
    ¾ cup finely chopped celery

Combine vinegar and spices. Fold into yogurt; cover and chill for several hours.

To prepare salad, coat apples with lemon juice. When ready to serve, mix dressing with apples, cabbages, and celery.

cheese and vegetable salad

Yield: 8 servings

    1 head Romaine, chopped
    ¼ cup crisp bacon, finely diced
    1 tablespoon Roquefort cheese,
        crumbled
    1 tablespoon low-fat cottage cheese
    3 tomatoes, peeled and diced
    1 avocado, peeled and diced
    2 hard-cooked egg whites,
        chopped finely

Mix ingredients well, cover, and refrigerate. Serve with Zero-Calorie Dressing (see Index).

sauerkraut salad with ham

sauerkraut salad with ham

Yield: 4 servings

1 16-ounce can sauerkraut
½ pound blue grapes
6 ounces cooked ham

dressing

½ cup yogurt
¼ teaspoon salt
¼ teaspoon white pepper
1 teaspoon honey

Rinse and drain sauerkraut; chop coarsely. Wash grapes and cut in half; remove seeds if desired. Cut ham in julienne strips. Gently mix these three ingredients.

Blend dressing ingredients and stir into sauerkraut mixture. Marinate for 10 minutes and adjust seasoning before serving if necessary.

feta-cheese salad

Yield: 4 servings

½ **pound feta cheese**
Freshly ground black pepper
    (about ½ teaspoon)
2 tablespoons vegetable oil
2 tablespoons white vinegar
3 stalks celery
10 pecans or walnuts
½ **teaspoon salt**

Cut cheese in thin slices and arrange in a shallow bowl. Sprinkle cheese generously with freshly ground black pepper. Drizzle 1 tablespoon each of the oil and vinegar over the cheese.

Clean celery stalks and cut in thin slices. Arrange on the cheese. Sprinkle with the nuts. Drizzle with the rest of the oil and vinegar and sprinkle with salt. Cover, and refrigerate for at least 1 hour. Mix well and correct seasoning, if necessary.

feta-cheese salad

crab-dressed salad

Yield: 4 to 6 servings

dressing

⅓ cup chili sauce
1 tablespoon finely cut scallions
2 teaspoons tarragon vinegar
2 teaspoons lemon juice
½ teaspoon salt
1½ cups plain yogurt
1 can (7½-ounce) king crab meat,
    drained and flaked

salad

1 bag (10-ounce) fresh spinach,
    washed, broken into bite-size
    pieces, and chilled
6 ounces (low-fat) mozzarella
    cheese, cut into strips
1 stalk celery, sliced
¼ cup chopped parsley
Cucumber slices
Tomato wedges
Ripe olives

Combine chili sauce, scallions, vinegar, lemon juice, and salt; fold in yogurt and crab meat. Cover and chill several hours. Prepare salad greens by tossing together spinach, cheese, celery, and parsley in a salad bowl. Garnish with cucumber slices, tomato wedges, and ripe olives.

Pass dressing separately to serve.

chef's salad

Yield: 4 servings

    ½ head Boston lettuce
    1 large tomato, cut in eighths
    ½ cucumber, cut in thin slices
    1 small onion, grated
    ½ green pepper, cut in thin strips
    ½ cup plain yogurt
    1 tablespoon lemon juice
    ½ teaspoon salt
    ⅛ teaspoon white pepper
    1 clove garlic, minced
    1 teaspoon chopped parsley
    1 teaspoon dried dill
    ½ cup cooked chicken, cut in
        julienne strips
    ½ cup chopped cooked ham
    ¼ cup low-fat mozzarella cheese,
        cut in julienne strips
    2 sardines, drained and cut in half
        lengthwise
    3 stuffed green olives, sliced

Wash lettuce and tear in bite-size pieces. Arrange on a salad platter with tomato, cucumber, onion, and green pepper. Cover and refrigerate while preparing the rest of the ingredients and the dressing.

Blend the yogurt with the lemon juice and season with salt, pepper, garlic, parsley, and dill. Pour dressing over the salad greens; arrange meats, cheese, and sardines on top. Garnish with sliced olives.

chef's salad

blue-cheese salad dressing

Yield: About 1 cup

¼ cup crumbled blue cheese
1 teaspoon lemon juice
½ teaspoon grated onion
1 cup plain yogurt

Mash cheese with fork. Add lemon juice, onion, and yogurt. Chill thoroughly. Serve with tossed green salad.

anchovy cheese salad dressing

Yield: 2¼ cups

2 cups low-fat cottage cheese
1 tablespoon lemon juice
¼ cup skim milk
½ teaspoon salt
6 anchovy fillets
1 teaspoon paprika
¼ teaspoon dry mustard

Place all ingredients in electric blender. Blend until creamy. Additional milk may be used if a thinner dressing is desired.

zero-calorie salad dressing

Yield: ½ cup

½ cup wine vinegar
½ clove garlic, crushed
¼ teaspoon tarragon

1 tablespoon chopped parsley
¼ teaspoon oregano
¼ teaspoon salt

Shake well and pour over salad. This may be stored in the refrigerator for several weeks.

breads

orange nut bread

Yield: 1 loaf

> **2 cups sifted white flour**
> **¾ cup sifted whole-wheat flour**
> **⅓ cup wheat germ**
> **½ cup sugar**
> **1 tablespoon baking powder**
> **½ teaspoon baking soda**
> **1 cup orange juice**
> **⅓ cup vegetable oil**
> **1 egg, beaten**
> **⅓ cup walnuts, chopped**
> **2 tablespoons grated orange rind**

Measure dry ingredients and sift together in a large bowl. Stir in the rest of the ingredients until blended well. Pour batter into a greased 9 × 5-inch bread pan. Bake for 55 to 60 minutes in a preheated 350°F oven. Check center with a cake tester or toothpick. Immediately remove bread from pan.

apricot bran loaf

Yield: 1 loaf

> **1 cup dried fruit (apricots, pears, prunes, or apples)**
> **Boiling water**
> **2 tablespoons sugar**
> **1½ cups sifted all-purpose flour**
> **½ cup sugar**
> **4 teaspoons baking powder**
> **½ teaspoon salt**
> **1½ cups whole-bran cereal**
> **1 cup skim milk**
> **2 eggs, slightly beaten**
> **⅓ cup vegetable oil**

Cut dried fruit into small pieces with scissors. Pour boiling water over the fruit to cover it, and soak for 10 minutes. Drain well. Stir 2 tablespoons sugar into the fruit.

Sift together the flour, ½ cup sugar, baking powder, and salt. Mix together the bran cereal, milk, eggs, and oil. Add cereal–egg mixture to the flour mixture and stir until moistened. Stir in the fruit and pour into a greased 9 × 5-inch bread pan. Bake in a preheated 350°F oven for 1 hour. Remove from pan and cool on a rack.

raisin and bran bread

Yield: 3 loaves

    **2 cups unbleached all-purpose
      flour**
1 cup whole-wheat flour
1 tablespoon toasted wheat germ
2 packages active dry yeast
**1 cup rolled oats (regular or
      quick-cooking)**
1 cup whole-bran cereal
1 cup seedless raisins
1½ cups low-fat cottage cheese
2 tablespoons vegetable oil
1 tablespoon salt
½ cup honey
2½ cups boiling water
**About 4½ cups additional
      unbleached all-purpose flour**

In a large mixing bowl stir together the 2 cups flour, the whole-wheat flour, wheat germ, and yeast. Set aside.

In a separate bowl combine the rolled oats, bran cereal, raisins, cottage cheese, oil, salt, and honey. Cover with the boiling water and stir until thoroughly mixed. Cool to lukewarm.

Add cottage cheese mixture to dry ingredients in mixer bowl. Beat ½ minute at lowest speed of electric mixer, scraping bowl constantly. Beat 3 minutes at highest speed. Stir in about 4½ more cups of flour by hand, until mixture forms a moderately stiff dough. Turn out onto floured board and knead until smooth and elastic, about 10 minutes.

Place in greased bowl, turning once to grease surface. Cover with a dampened towel and let rise until double in bulk, about 1 hour. Punch down; divide into thirds. Cover, and let rest 10 minutes. Shape into 3 loaves.

Place in 3 greased 8½ × 4½ × 2½-inch loaf pans. Brush tops lightly with vegetable oil. Cover, and let rise until double, about 35 to 45 minutes. Bake in a 375°F oven 35 to 40 minutes, or until golden brown. Remove bread from pans and let cool on rack.

beverages

lemon cocktail

lemon cocktail

Yield: 1 serving

Juice of 1 lemon
Juice of ½ orange
1 teaspoon honey
2 jiggers sherry
3 ice cubes
1 lemon slice
1 orange slice
2 maraschino cherries

Shake lemon juice, orange juice, honey, and sherry in a cocktail shaker. Crush ice cubes and place in a tall glass. Pour lemon cocktail over ice. Peel lemon and orange slices, cut into small pieces, and add to drink. Garnish with cherries, and serve.

fruit tea punch

Yield: About 10 cups

    2 cups boiling water
    4 tea bags black tea
    ¼ cup lemon juice
    2 cups orange juice
    1 tablespoon honey
    1 lemon
    2 oranges
    2 cups fresh strawberries
    1 bottle soda water

fruit tea punch

Pour boiling water over tea bags and steep for 3 minutes; remove tea bags. Blend in lemon and orange juice and sweeten with honey.

Cut peel from lemon and oranges, and section fruit. Remove all membranes. Add fruit to tea. Wash and hull strawberries and cut in half; add to tea. Cover and refrigerate punch for at least 6 hours to blend flavors. Just before serving, add bottle of soda water.

apple-grape fruit salad

apple–grape fruit salad

Yield: 4 servings

2 medium tart apples, peeled, quartered, and cored
½ pound blue grapes, halved and seeded

1 stalk garden mint (leaves only)
2 teaspoons sugar
2 tablespoons lemon juice
2 tablespoons brandy

Cut apples crosswise in thin slices. Arrange grapes, apples, and mint leaves in a glass bowl. Sprinkle with sugar, lemon juice, and brandy. Toss lightly. Cover, and chill 1 hour.

ambrosia

Yield: 6 to 8 servings

3 oranges, peeled and sectioned
2 bananas, peeled and sliced
    diagonally
½ teaspoon lemon juice
2 cups strawberries, washed and
    hulled

1 small cantaloupe, peeled, seeded,
    and sliced
1 papaya, peeled, seeded, and
    sliced (optional)
½ cup flaked coconut

Sprinkle lemon juice on bananas to prevent darkening. Arrange fruits in individual serving dishes. Sprinkle coconut over the tops.

baked prune puff

Yield: 6 servings

2 cups cooked prunes
¼ cup sugar
2 tablespoons orange juice

½ teaspoon grated orange peel
½ teaspoon cinnamon
4 egg whites

Pit prunes and mash to a pulp. Add 2 tablespoons of the sugar, the orange juice, peel, and cinnamon. Blend thoroughly.

Beat egg whites until foamy and add the remaining 2 tablespoons sugar. Continue beating until stiff. Gently fold prune mixture into beaten egg whites.

Pile lightly in a greased 1½-quart casserole dish. Bake in a preheated 350°F oven for 20 to 30 minutes.

blancmange

Yield: 4 servings

3 tablespoons cornstarch
⅓ cup sugar
¼ teaspoon salt

¼ cup cold skim milk
2 cups hot skim milk
1 teaspoon vanilla

In the top of a double boiler mix cornstarch, sugar, and salt. Add cold milk and stir until smooth. Add hot milk gradually and cook for 15 minutes, stirring constantly, until the mixture thickens. Add flavoring. Chill.

pears with raspberry sauce

Yield: 4 servings

4 large fresh pears
3 cups water
1 cinnamon stick
2 whole cloves
2-inch piece of lemon peel
3 tablespoons honey

6 tablespoons low-fat cottage
  cheese
1 tablespoon lemon juice
1 10-ounce package frozen whole
  raspberries
4 teaspoons sliced almonds

Peel pears, but do not remove stems. Cut pears in half and carefully remove cores.

In a saucepan, add water, cinnamon stick, cloves, lemon peel, and 2 tablespoons of the honey; bring to a boil. Add pears and simmer for 10 minutes. Remove pears with a slotted spoon and drain.

Puree cottage cheese in a blender. Spoon into a bowl and stir in lemon juice and 1 tablespoon honey. Adjust sweetness to your taste.

Fill pear halves with cottage cheese mixture and arrange 2 pear halves upright on a dish to form 1 whole pear. If necessary, cut a small slice from the bottoms of the pears to make them stand up.

Puree raspberries, reserving a few whole berries for garnish. Pour over pears. Sprinkle pears with almonds and garnish with reserved berries.

pears with raspberry sauce

lemon sherbet

Yield: 6 servings

1½ teaspoons unflavored gelatin
2 tablespoons cold water
2 cups skim milk
¾ cup sugar

½ cup lemon juice
½ teaspoon grated lemon rind
2 egg whites, stiffly beaten

Soak gelatin in 2 tablespoons cold water for several minutes.

Heat milk; add sugar and gelatin. Stir until dissolved. Chill in the refrigerator until mixture is just starting to become firm. Gradually stir in the lemon juice and lemon rind. Pour into a freezing tray and freeze to a mush.

Turn into a chilled bowl and beat with an electric beater until fluffy, but not melted. Fold in egg whites and return to the freezing unit. Freeze until firm.

apricot sherbet

Yield: 6 servings

3 cups apricot nectar
1 cup canned water-packed
    apricots, chopped

1 3-ounce package lemon gelatin
    dessert powder
1 tablespoon lemon juice

Mix all ingredients in a saucepan. Heat until gelatin powder is completely dissolved. Freeze until partially frozen. Whip with electric mixer and return to freezer to set.

strawberry–pineapple dessert

Yield: 6 servings

1 package strawberry-flavored gelatin
1 cup hot water
¾ cup canned pineapple juice
⅛ teaspoon salt

1 egg white
6 fresh or frozen strawberries for
    garnish

Dissolve gelatin in hot water. Add the pineapple juice and salt. Chill in the refrigerator until mixture has started to thicken. Add the egg white and whip with an electric beater until fluffy and thick.

Divide mixture among six dessert glasses. Chill until firm. Garnish with strawberries.

index